LEARNING
TO
WRITE FICTION
FROM THE
MASTERS

Barnaby Conrad

A PLUME BOOK

PLUME
Published by the Penguin Group
Penguin Books USA Inc., 375 Hudson Street,
New York, New York 10014, U.S.A.
Penguin Books Ltd, 27 Wrights Lane, London W8 5TZ, England
Penguin Books Australia Ltd, Ringwood, Victoria, Australia
Penguin Books Canada Ltd, 10 Alcorn Avenue,
Toronto, Ontario, Canada M4V 3B2
Penguin Books (N.Z.) Ltd, 182–190 Wairau Road, Auckland 10, New Zealand

Penguin Books Ltd, Registered Offices:
Harmondsworth, Middlesex, England

First published by Plume, an imprint of Dutton Signet,
a division of Penguin Books USA Inc.

First Printing, June, 1996
10 9 8 7 6 5 4 3 2 1

Grateful Acknowledgments to:

Harcourt Brace & Co. for excerpts from *Pale Horse, Pale Rider*, Katherine A. Porter in *Pale Horse, Pale Rider, Three Short Novels*, copyright 1937 and renewed 1965 by Katherine Anne Porter, reprinted by permission of Harcourt Brace & Company.

Michael Imison Playwrights Ltd, 28 Almeida Street, London N1 1TD, for *Private Lives*, copyright 1930, the Estate of Noel Coward

Viking Penguin, for "A Telephone Call" by Dorothy Parker from *The Portable Dorothy Parker*, introduction by Brendan Gill. Copyright 1928, renewed © 1956 by Dorothy Parker. Used by Permission of Viking Penguin, a division of Penguin Books USA Inc.; *A Gun for Sale*, by Graham Greene. Copyright 1936 by Graham Greene, renewed. Used by permission of Viking Penguin, a division of Penguin Books USA Inc.; and "A Shocking Accident," copyright © 1957 by Graham Greene, from *Collected Stories of Graham Greene*. Used by permission of Viking Penguin, a division of Penguin Books USA Inc.

Patricia Powell and Harold Ober, for *I'm a Fool*, Sherwood Anderson. Reprinted by permission of Harold Ober Associates Incorporated. Copyright © 1922 the Dial Publishing Company, Inc. Renewed 1949 by Eleanor Copenhaver Anderson.

Farrar, Straus & Giroux, for an excerpt from "Everything That Rises Must Converge" from *The Complete Stories of Flannery O'Connor*. Copyright © 1965,

(The following page constitutes an extension of this copyright page.)

"All professional writers will applaud Barnaby Conrad's advice to beginners—'If you want to write well, you must read widely.' " —James A. Michener

- F. Scott Fitzgerald shows one way of starting a novel with his marvelous opening of *Tender Is the Night*.
- Dashiell Hammet illustrates a spare style like a razor-sharp etching tool to create character when Sam Spade meets "the fat man" in *The Maltese Falcon*.
- Charlotte Brontë brilliantly intensifies the fires of passionate romance when Jane Eyre first meets Rochester in the novel that bears the immortal heroine's name.
- Graham Greene constructs a scene of overwhelmingly powerful action in the assassination of a political leader in *This Gun for Hire*.

These are but a few of the great writers and unforgettable scenes that Barnaby Conrad has chosen to open new vistas of writing possibility and new dimensions of technical understanding for aspiring writers. Anyone who is serious about making the most of his or her talent and vision by putting the right words in the right order on a blank page will find these masterful examples, together with Conrad's comments on them, to be immensely inspiring as well as instructive.

MASTER WRITERS DEMONSTRATE WHAT THEY DO BEST

Barnaby Conrad, at one time a private secretary to Sinclair Lewis, has written more than two dozen books, including the bestselling novel *Matador*. Co-founder and director of the Santa Barbara Writers Conference, now in its twenty-fourth year, the multitalented Mr. Conrad has yet another career as an artist and formerly taught painting at the University of California at Santa Barbara.

FOR MICHAEL LARSEN,
WHOSE IDEA IT WAS. . . .

By speech first, but far more by writing, man has been able to put something of himself beyond death. In tradition and in books an integral part of the individual persists, for it can influence the minds and actions of other people in different places and at different times: a row of black marks on a page can move a man to tears, though the bones of him that wrote it are long ago crumbled to dust.

—JULIAN HUXLEY

We work in the dark—we do what we can—we give what we have. Our doubt is our passion, and our passion is our task. The rest is the madness of art.

—HENRY JAMES

CONTENTS

PREFACE

"I haven't read the book—but I saw the movie!"

This is a statement we hear a distressing number of times during the annual Santa Barbara Writers Conference. I have nothing against films—I love films—but they are not books.

It has been said, perhaps facetiously, that one American in 20,000 reads a book a year, but that *two* Americans in 20,000 are *writing* a book.

Everyone will agree that the only way to learn to write is by reading and writing.

I am amazed at how little most of the aspirant writers I meet have read. They often seem unacquainted with the writings in the very genre they intend to invade. If, for example, they wish to write detective stories it would seem to me to be helpful if not imperative to have read as much as possible of Poe, Conan Doyle, Hammett, Christie, Sayers, Chandler, Cain, Macdonald, Rendell, P. D. James, and Grafton, among many others.

One of the objectives of this book is to expose would-be writers to passages from authors of acknowledged mastery that especially pertain to certain situations and elements of storytelling. Seeing how the masters handle these scenes might inspire beginning authors to resolve their own specific writing problems.

CHAPTER ONE

BEGINNINGS

When I was twenty-four I worked for the famous novelist Sinclair Lewis for six months as a secretary-chauffeur-protégé. A great deal of what I learned from him permeates this book.

One of his maxims was:

Never make your protagonist a bore! A villain, a murderer, a rapist, a child molester, a cheat, a womanizer, perhaps, but never a bore. And if he is merely an accountant, make him a good one.

He then told me how he once set out to write a novel "about the most boring man in the world. I succeeded admirably, but at the same time I also managed to write the most boring book in the world."

The novel was *The Man Who Knew Coolidge*, and Lewis told me about how he obtained firsthand, visual proof of just how boring it was. He was on the way to Europe on the *Queen Elizabeth* when, one day, he was pleased to see a woman settle into a deck chair and open a copy of the just-published novel. His joy was short-lived, however, when he watched her read the first page, then walk to the rail and drop the book over the side of the ship.

"If I didn't already know it," Lewis told me, "I learned then that the first page—even the first sentence—of one's article, short story, novel, or nonfiction book is of paramount importance."

Lewis, America's first Nobel Prize winner in literature, was a consummate craftsman, and we can learn from him—as well as from other masters—how to begin a novel or a short story in a way that will catch the reader's (or more important, the editor's) attention. Remember, when an editor takes your piece out of its manila envelope, you will not be there at his elbow to say: "Keep reading! It gets really good later on— terrific scene coming up!"

There'll be no "later on" if the editor is not intrigued right off the bat. He or she does not necessarily have to be shocked, startled, or amazed, but the editor, putting himself in the place of a reader, must be tantalized enough to read further. A well-drafted opening immediately tells the editor that he is dealing with a good writer; professional writers seldom write a dull first page of a novel or short story.

We can break down the various ways of starting an article or a story or a novel into twelve general categories. In the old days these categories might have been applied only to fiction, but nowadays the boundaries between fiction and nonfiction have become blurred.

Let's look at those categories one by one:

1. SETTING

In the past, when people had more time and there was no TV, no film, novels almost invariably started with a purely physical description: a New England drawing room, perhaps, an Alpine meadow, a western landscape, or a dark and stormy night in London. Some writers who wish to give the reader an immediate sense of place and mood still prefer to open with description. By and large, static description is more appropriate for book-length fiction.

In his writing workshops, Donald Barthelme used to pound the table and declare emphatically to his students: "No weather, *please*!"

But if you choose to begin by describing weather or scenery or by, say, taking inventory of a parlor, you must write very well if you are to engage the attention of the reader.

Here is the masterful opening by F. Scott Fitzgerald of his 1933 novel *Tender Is the Night*:

On the pleasant shore of the French Riviera, about half way between Marseilles and the Italian border, stands a large, proud, rose-colored hotel. Deferential palms cool its flushed façade, and before it stretches a short dazzling beach. Lately it has become a summer resort of notable and fashionable people; a decade ago it was almost deserted after its English clientele went north in April. Now, many bungalows cluster near it, but when this story begins only the cupolas of a dozen old villas rotted like water lilies among the massed pines between Gausse's Hôtel des Étrangers and Cannes, five miles away.

The hotel and its bright tan prayer rug of a beach were one. In the early morning the distant image of Cannes, the pink and cream of old fortifications, the purple Alp that bounded Italy, were cast across the water and lay quavering in the ripples and rings sent up by sea-plants through the clear shallows. Before eight a man came down to the beach in a blue bathrobe and with much preliminary application to his person of the chilly water, and much grunting and loud breathing, floundered a minute in the sea. When he had gone, beach and bay were quiet for an hour. Merchantmen crawled westward on the horizon; bus boys shouted in the hotel court; the dew dried upon the pines. In another hour the horns of motors began to blow down from the winding road along the low range of the Maures, which separates the littoral from true Provençal France.

A mile from the sea, where pines give way to dusty poplars, is an isolated railroad stop, whence one June morning in 1925 a victoria brought a woman and her daughter down to Gausse's Hotel. The mother's face was of a fading prettiness that would soon be patted with broken veins; her expression was both tranquil and aware in a pleasant way. However, one's eye moved on quickly to her daughter, who had magic in her pink palms and her cheeks lit to a lovely flame, like the thrilling flush of children after their cold baths in the evening. Her fine forehead sloped gently up to where her hair, bordering it like an armorial shield, burst into lovelocks and waves and curlicues of ash blonde and gold. Her eyes were bright, big, clear, wet, and shining, the color of her cheeks was real, breaking close to the surface from the strong young pump of her heart. Her body hovered delicately on the last edge of childhood—she was almost eighteen, nearly complete, but the dew was still on her.

As sea and sky appeared below them in a thin, hot line the mother said:

"Something tells me we're not going to like this place."

Although the author begins with a static description that in lesser hands might be self-indulgent and boring, here the language, the imagery, the specific details, the carefully selected verbs all combine to tell us instantly that we are in good hands and that we should read on. And sure enough, in the third paragraph Fitzgerald rewards us by introducing two important characters: "a victoria brought a woman and her daughter down to Gausse's Hotel."

And talk about foreshadowing and hint of conflict—note

the artful line: "Something tells me we're not going to like this place." We *must* continue reading to find out what is going to happen that will cause them to not like the place.

As long as we have that nice example of description by Fitzgerald in front of us, let's also note his use throughout of vigorous, cliché-free verbs, ones that help us *see* what the writer wants us to see more clearly: cool, cluster, rotted, quavering, floundered, crawled, dried, patted.

We will address the enormous importance of verbs at length in a later chapter, but back to beginnings and another category.

2. SETTING PLUS CHARACTERS

A more common, economical, and exciting way to begin is by combining *characters with setting*.

By using this combination the writer reveals something about a character, as well as describing the place that the plot is to be played out, and may even suggest a hint of the conflict to come.

I'll make up an example. Instead of simply describing a setting sun in detail, let's open with the protagonist watching and reacting to that sunset:

> Norman watched as the dying sun gilded his beloved log house and the barn and his horse, and his gut twisted at the thought he might lose it all. And up there in those beautiful blue hills were two men and a bitter woman who wanted to see him dead.

Here a wary protagonist is shown in a specific setting, with something happening—the reader does not yet know what. But the reader will read on. Who is doing what to whom?

One might suppose that Emily Brontë would begin her famous 1847 novel *Wuthering Heights* with a plummy, lush description of the purple, heather-festooned moors that she loved and which play such an important part in the background of the romance between her protagonists, Cathy and Heathcliff.

Not at all; she is too fine a storyteller not to want to get things moving right away, to introduce her pivotal character, and to let us know we're in for a bumpy ride.

> I have just returned from a visit to my landlord—the solitary neighbour that I shall be troubled with. This is certainly a beautiful country! In all England, I do not believe that I could have fixed on a situation so completely removed from the stir of society. A perfect misanthropist's heaven; and Mr. Heathcliff and I are such a suitable pair to divide the desolation between us. A capital fellow! He little imagined how my heart warmed towards him when I beheld his black eyes withdraw so suspiciously under their brows, as I rode up, and when his fingers sheltered themselves, with a jealous resolution, still further in his waistcoat, as I announced my name.
>
> "Mr. Heathcliff!" I said.
>
> A nod was the answer.

This splendid opening is worth several readings, containing as it does so much information, subtle characterization, and hints of conflict to come. There is a nod to the setting ("beautiful country!"—"so removed"—"desolation"), but it is the sly description of the "solitary neighbour" that engages the attention of Brontë—and her reader ("misanthropist's heaven"— "black eyes withdraw so suspiciously under their brows"— "fingers sheltered themselves"—"jealous resolution").

This is a man to approach with caution and not for a moment do we subscribe to the narrator's pronouncement that he is a "capital fellow."

Notice how Brontë introduces conflict, hence interest, in her very first sentence—"that I shall be troubled with."
Troubled. That is the essence of every story and every novel—trouble, problems, conflict. And no one knew it better than Emily Brontë. Let us see how she proceeds with her story, first having her narrator introduce himself to Heathcliff—and to the reader.

"Mr. Lockwood, your new tenant, sir. I do myself the honour of calling as soon as possible after my arrival, to express the hope that I have not inconvenienced you by my perseverance in soliciting the occupation of Thrushcross Grange: I heard yesterday you had had some thoughts—"

"Thrushcross Grange is my own, sir," he interrupted wincing. "I should not allow any one to inconvenience me, if I could hinder it—walk in!"

The "walk in" was uttered with closed teeth, and expressed the sentiment, "Go to the deuce": even the gate over which he leant manifested no sympathising movement to the words; and I think that circumstance determined me to accept the invitation: I felt interested in a man who seemed more exaggeratedly reserved than myself.

When he saw my horse's breast fairly pushing the barrier, he did put out his hand to unchain it, and then suddenly preceded me up the causeway, calling, as we entered the court—"Joseph, take Mr. Lockwood's horse; and bring up some wine."

"Here we have the whole establishment of domestics, I suppose," was the reflection suggested by this compound order. "No wonder the grass grows up between the flags, and cattle are the only hedgecutters."

Joseph was an elderly, nay, an old man: very old, perhaps, though hale and sinewy. "The Lord help us!" he soliloquised in an undertone of peevish displeasure, while relieving me of my horse: looking, meantime, in my face so sourly that I charitably conjectured he must have need of divine aid to digest his dinner, and his pious ejaculation had no reference to my unexpected advent.

Observe the subtle words implying an uncomfortable situation—*conflict*: "interrupted wincing"—"closed teeth"—"go to the deuce"—"no sympathising movement"—"peevish displeasure"—"so sourly."

Remember, *amiability is the enemy of a story*!

Now, having introduced us to three characters and created a mood which intrigues us as to what might happen in the next pages, the author feels she can indulge herself in describing the setting in great detail, yet never straying too far away from the prickly presence and character of the mysterious landlord:

Wuthering Heights is the name of Mr. Heathcliff's dwelling. "Wuthering" being a significant provincial adjective, descriptive of the atmospheric tumult to which its station is exposed in stormy weather. Pure, bracing ventilation they must have up there at all times, indeed: one may guess the power of the north wind blowing over the edge, by the excessive slant of a few stunted firs at the end of the house; and by a range of gaunt thorns all stretching their limbs one way, as if craving alms of the sun. Happily, the architect had foresight to build it strong: the narrow windows are deeply set in the wall, and the corners defended with large jutting stones.

Before passing the threshold, I paused to admire a quantity of grotesque carving lavished over the front, and especially about the principal door; above which, among a wilderness of crumbling griffins and shameless little boys, I detected the date "1500," and the name "Hareton Earnshaw." I would have made a few comments, and requested a short history of the place from the surly owner:

but his attitude at the door appeared to demand my speedy entrance, or complete departure, and I had no desire to aggravate his impatience previous to inspecting the pene-tralium.

One step brought us into the family sitting-room, without any introductory lobby or passage: they call it here "the house" pre-eminently. It includes kitchen and parlour, generally; but I believe at Wuthering Heights the kitchen is forced to retreat altogether into another quarter: at least I distinguished a chatter of tongues, and a clatter of culinary utensils, deep within; and I observed no signs of roasting, boiling, or baking, about the huge fire-place; nor any glitter of copper saucepans and tin cullenders on the walls. One end, indeed, reflected splendidly both light and heat from ranks of immense pewter dishes, interspersed with silver jugs and tankards, towering row after row, on a vast oak dresser, to the very roof. The latter had never been underdrawn: its entire anatomy lay bare to an enquiring eye, except where a frame of wood laden with oatcakes and clusters of legs of beef, mutton, and ham, concealed it. Above the chimney were sundry villainous old guns, and a couple of horse-pistols: and, by way of ornament, three gaudily-painted canisters disposed along its ledge. The floor was of smooth white stone; the chairs, high-backed, primitive structures, painted green: one or two heavy black ones lurking in the shade. In an arch under the dresser, reposed a huge, liver-coloured bitch pointer, surrounded by a swarm of squealing puppies; and other dogs haunted other recesses.

The apartment and furniture would have been nothing extraordinary as belonging to a homely, northern farmer, with a stubborn countenance, and stalwart limbs set out to advantage in knee-breeches and gaiters. Such an individual seated in his arm-chair, his mug of ale frothing on the round table before him, is to be seen in any circuit of five or six miles among these hills, if you go at the right time after dinner. But Mr. Heathcliff forms a singular contrast to his abode and style of living. He is a dark-skinned gipsy in aspect, in dress and manners a gentleman: that is, as much a gentleman as many a country squire: rather slovenly, perhaps, yet not looking amiss with his negligence, because he has an erect and handsome figure; and rather morose. Possibly, some people might suspect him of a degree of under-bred pride; I have a sympathetic chord within that tells me it is nothing of the sort: I know, by instinct, his reserve springs from an aversion to showy displays of feeling—to manifestations of mutual kindliness. He'll love and hate equally under cover, and esteem it a species of impertinence to be loved or hated again.

Masterful writing by a master writer!

3. THEMATIC

A method of beginning a story opposite to starting with a happening is to start off with a philosophical idea, or truism, or generality. Here is an example from Jane Austen's *Pride and Prejudice*:

It is a truth universally acknowledged that a single man in possession of a good fortune must be in want of a wife.

Then there is Tolstoy's famous opening line from *Anna Karenina*:

Happy families are all alike; every unhappy family is unhappy in its own way.

That is such an arresting thought that we wish to hear more from the person who voiced it, so we read on; as with the opening of Michael Chabon's recent story "Ocean Avenues" in *The New Yorker*:

> If you can still see how you could once have loved a person, you are still in love; an extinct love is always wholly incredible. One day not too long ago, in Laguna Beach ...

The writer wants you to say to yourself: "Sure, that's happened to me too. I'll read on." As with the astute observation by Somerset Maugham in the first sentence of *Cakes and Ale*, written in 1932:

> I have noticed that when someone asks for you on the telephone and, finding you out, leaves a message begging you to call him up the moment you come in, as it's important, the matter is more often important to him than to you.

Scott Fitzgerald began his long story "The Rich Boy" with a valuable thought for writers and then more generalization:

> Begin with an individual, and before you know it you find that you have created a type; begin with a type, and you find that you have created—nothing. That is because we are all queer fish, queerer behind our faces and voices than we want any one to know or than we know ourselves. When I hear a man proclaiming himself an "average, honest, open fellow," I feel pretty sure that he has some definite and perhaps terrible abnormality which he has agreed to conceal—and his protestation of being average and honest and open is his way of reminding himself of his misprision.

Do you know what all five of these disparate beginnings have in common?

The answer is that, after indulging very briefly in generalizations, the authors immediately shifted gears and plunged into *a specific happening* so as to involve the reader in the forthcoming story as soon as possible.

4. FACTUAL

A factual type of beginning should be an attention grabber whether for a fiction or a nonfiction work, as in this realistic, no-nonsense opening I've made up for an article on the Chernobyl disaster:

On April 26, 1986, an explosion in Unit No. 4 at the Chernobyl nuclear power station set the reactor's graphite core ablaze, jeopardizing the entire reactor complex and spewing into the winds radioactive debris that threatened human health and the food chain even beyond the vast area of Ukraine. More than thirty of the reactor operators, guards, and local firemen who fought to contain the damage and extinguish the fire died from radiation poisoning.

An equally effective beginning about the disaster could borrow from fictional techniques using dialogue:

"God, it was so terrible and I was so scared," said Natasha Trompesky, an elderly survivor of Chernobyl. "I felt the ground tremble and heard the noise and I thought of my husband still inside."

Hemingway, a former journalist, liked the factual-sounding beginning for his fiction; witness *The Old Man and the Sea*'s first sentence:

He was an old man who fished alone in a skiff in the Gulf Stream and he had gone eighty-four days now without taking a fish.

Who, where, what, when in one sentence!

In "The Snows of Kilimanjaro," one of the best-known American short stories, Hemingway places this factual-appearing but enigmatic item above the title:

> Kilimanjaro is a snow-covered mountain 19,710 feet high, and is said to be the highest mountain in Africa. Its western summit is called the Masai "Ngàje Ngài," the House of God. Close to the western summit there is the dried and frozen carcass of a leopard. No one has explained what the leopard was seeking at that altitude.

Nor does Hemingway attempt to explain the leopard's presence in the story. But we are hooked!

Then there is the purely factual beginning for the purely factual article or book. A couple of years ago the *New York Times* asked a dozen famous writers what their favorite beginning to a book was. Elmore Leonard, the great suspense writer, picked the factual beginning of my book *La Fiesta Brava*:

> On August 28, 1947, a multi-millionaire and a bull killed each other in Linares, Spain, and plunged an entire nation into deep mourning. The bull's name was Islero, and he was of the Miura strain. The man's name was Manolete, and he was the essence of everything Spanish.

There is also the seemingly factual, straightforward, no-nonsense statement that sets the tone of the entire work, as in Norman MacLean's *A River Runs Through It* (and, indeed, a river does run all through the novel):

> In our family, there was no clear line between religion and fly fishing. We lived at the junction of great trout riv-

ers in western Montana, and our father was a Presbyterian minister and a fly fisherman who tied his own flies and taught others. He told us about Christ's disciples being fishermen, and we were left to assume, as my brother and I did, that all first-class fishermen on the Sea of Galilee were fly fishermen and that John, the favorite, was a dry-fly fisherman.

5. EMOTIONAL: AIM FOR THE HEART!

Beginnings that appeal immediately and directly to a reader's emotions are among the most successful, whether fiction or nonfiction. Take staff writer Alan Abrahamson's lead in a *Los Angeles Times* account of a real-life murder:

> On a pleasant autumn afternoon in Northridge, Froggy, Chunky, and Nini killed the neighbor lady.
>
> Chunky and Nini, who were 15 and 12, stabbed her 11 times. Their sister Froggy, 16, stayed at home and turned up the volume on the family's two stereos to drown out the screams from next door.
>
> The neighbor, 62-year-old librarian Meta Frances Murphy, had befriended the girls, often treating them to snacks or driving them to and from school. It was a crime that made no sense—and still doesn't.

How could one not read on?

An emotion-evoking beginning in fiction is a surefire way of luring the reader into your story or novel. How about this one, from Ambrose Bierce's classic short story "An Imperfect Conflagration":

> Early one morning in 1872 I murdered my father—an act which made a deep impression on me at the time.

Almost 100 years after that was written, Allan Folsom's hugely successful 1994 thriller *The Day After Tomorrow* starts out:

> Paul Osborn sat alone among the smoky bustle of the after-work crowd, staring into a glass of red wine. He was tired and hurt and confused. For no particular reason he looked up. When he did, his breath left him with a jolt. Across the room sat the man who murdered his father. . . .

The reason this strikes an immediate chord in the reader, of course, is that subconsciously we wonder how *we* would react and what would *we* do if we encountered a person who had murdered one of our parents.

Writers can also arouse emotions in the reader subtly and quietly, as does the opening sentence of Mary McCarthy's *The Company She Keeps*:

> She would leave him, she thought, as soon as the petunias bloomed.

Or Gabriel García Márquez's arresting first sentence in his 1967 novel *One Hundred Years of Solitude*:

> Many years later, as he faced the firing squad, Colonel Aureliano Buendía was to remember that distant afternoon when his father took him to discover ice.

For a more brazen attention getter here's Mary Breasted's outrageous lead into her novel *Why Should You Doubt Me Now?*:

> If there is a fate that can befall a man worse than having the Virgin Mary appear in his bedroom just as he is about to seduce the most beautiful apprentice horoscope writer in Dublin, Rupert Penrole did not know of one.

6. ACTION

Action beginnings are effective because of the all-important fact that *Action is character!* as Scott Fitzgerald told us so emphatically so long ago.

By action we mean any significant movement, endeavor, activity, or event engaged in by people (or, in some cases, animals).

The action may be violent, as in the opening of Ambrose Bierce's "An Occurrence at Owl Creek Bridge," where a young man is about to be hanged:

> A man stood upon a railroad bridge in northern Alabama, looking down into the swift water twenty feet below. The man's hands were behind his back, the wrists bound with a cord. A rope closely encircled his neck.

Or a projected murder as in Richard North Patterson's novel *The Lasko Tangent*:

> It was the Monday morning before they killed him. I didn't know then that he existed. Or that I would help change that.

James M. Cain's beginning to his 1934 novel, *The Postman Always Rings Twice*, influenced many writers of the era:

> They threw me off the hay truck about noon.

But the story or article can also start with action as simple as a Little League game or a church wedding, or a birth, or a telephone call, or an anniversary, or a fraternity party, or a riparian picnic, or a graduation, or a knock at the door, or a funeral. Or an arduous trek, as in Jack London's short-story masterpiece, "To Build a Fire":

Day had broken cold and grey, exceedingly cold and grey, when the man turned aside from the main Yukon trail and climbed the high earth-bank, where a dim and little-traveled trail led eastward through the fat spruce timberland. It was a steep bank, and he paused for breath at the top, excusing the act to himself by looking at his watch.

7. IN MEDIAS RES

Rather than setting the scene or describing the situation in detail beforehand, the writer plunges the reader directly "into the middle of things." Here is Frederick Forsyth's beginning of *The Day of the Jackal*:

It is cold at 6:40 in the morning of a March day in Paris, and seems even colder when a man is about to be executed by firing squad. At that hour on March 11, 1963, in the main courtyard of the Ford d'Jury a French Air Force colonel stood before a stake driven into the chilly gravel as his hands were bound behind the post, and stared with slowly diminishing disbelief at the squad of soldiers facing him twenty metres away.

We don't know who the man is or what he has done to deserve execution or whether the sentence will be carried out.

But! . . . we want to find out. And that, after all, is the name of the game.

Robert Ludlum, Elmore Leonard, Mary Higgins Clark, Robert Parker, Ed McBain, and Sue Grafton, to name a few among many other best-selling novelists, also favor the *in medias res* beginning. In the how-*medias-res*-can-you-get department, here is Eudora Welty:

I remember a sentence I opened a story with:

Monsieur Boule inserted a delicate dagger in Mademoiselle's left side and departed with a poised immediacy.

I like to think I didn't take myself seriously then, but I did.

8. DIALOGUE

Everyone practices—and enjoys—eavesdropping, especially if the subject and person speaking are interesting and exciting. Readers, therefore, respond immediately to a story (or article) that starts with people talking, particularly if there is tension or conflict in their dialogue. For example from yesterday's newspaper:

"I didn't realize the gun was loaded," mumbled a distraught Mark Smith yesterday outside his Brentwood home.

His neighbor, Juan Gomez, restrained by friends, shouted: "You'll pay for this, you weasel! Ask that girl who says she's your wife!"

Having caught our attention, the writer gives the facts of the situation.

Here are some diverse examples of stories that begin with dialogue; they have nothing in common except that they provoke our interest or tell us something about the protagonist or simply get the story going:

Aldous Huxley's "The Giaconda Smile":

"Miss Spence will be down directly, sir."

"Thank you," said Mr. Hutton, without turning around. Janet Spence's parlourmaid was so ugly—ugly on purpose, it always seemed to him, malignantly, criminally ugly—that he could not bear to look at her more than was necessary.

Eudora Welty's "Petrified Man":

"Reach in my purse and git me a cigarette without no powder in it if you kin, Mrs. Fletcher, honey," said Leota to her ten o'clock shampoo-and-set customer. "I don't like no perfumed cigarettes."

Hemingway likes to start with dialogue, then let the reader know who is talking and what the situation is, as in "The Snows of Kilimanjaro." This conversation comes immediately after the little squib about the dead leopard and the title:

"The marvellous thing is that it's painless," he said. "That's how you know when it starts."
"Is it really?"
"Absolutely. I'm awfully sorry about the odor though. That must bother you."
"Don't! Please don't."
"Look at them," he said. "Now is it sight or is it scent that brings them like that?"
The cot the man lay on was in the wide shade of a mimosa tree and as he looked out past the shade onto the glare of the plain there were three of the big birds squatted obscenely, while in the sky a dozen more sailed, making quick-moving shadows as they passed.

9. CHARACTERIZATION

Starting with a description of a protagonist or antagonist is valid. Observe this opening from a famous novel:

Scarlett O'Hara was not beautiful, but men seldom realized it when caught by her charm as the Tarleton twins were.

This not only introduces our heroine but takes us firmly into the first scene of Margaret Mitchell's epic book.

To begin *Lord Jim*, Joseph Conrad gives the reader an immediate and graphic physical description of his character and, at the same time, works in some of the man's character and profession:

> He was an inch, perhaps two, under six feet, powerfully built, and he advanced straight at you with a slight stoop of the shoulders, head forward, and a fixed-from-under stare which made you think of a charging bull. His voice was deep, loud, and his manner displayed a kind of dogged self-assertion which had nothing aggressive in it. It seemed a necessity, and it was directed apparently as much at himself as at anybody else. He was spotlessly neat, apparelled in immaculate white from shoes to hat, and in the various Eastern ports where he got his living as ship-chandler's water-clerk he was very popular.

In this flamboyant beginning Vladimir Nabokov characterizes the narrator as well as his young—very young—heroine, the eponymous Lolita:

> Lolita, light of my life, fire of my loins. My sin, my soul. Lo-lee-ta: the tip of the tongue taking a trip of three steps down the palate to tap, at three, on the teeth. Lo. Lee. Ta.
>
> She was Lo, plain Lo, in the morning, standing four feet ten in one sock. She was Lola in slacks. She was Dolly at school. She was Dolores on the dotted line. But in my arms she was always Lolita.
>
> Did she have a precursor? She did, indeed she did. In point of fact, there might have been no Lolita at all had I not loved, one summer, a certain initial girl-child. In a princedom by the sea. Oh when? About as many years be-

fore Lolita was born as my age was that summer. You can always count on a murderer for a fancy prose style.

Ladies and gentlemen of the jury, exhibit number one is what the seraphs, the misinformed, simple, noble-winged seraphs, envied. Look at this tangle of thorns.

10. AUTHOR-TO-READER

"Call me Ishmael," Herman Melville's narrator warmly invites the reader in *Moby-Dick.*

This is a disarming, confidential, effective, and somewhat old-fashioned way to begin a story. The writer addresses the reader directly. Here is Edgar Allan Poe seemingly confiding in the reader as he begins his chilling tale "The Tell-Tale Heart":

True!—nervous—very, very dreadfully nervous I had been and am! But why will you say that I am mad?

Study Mark Twain's chatty—and artful—opening to *The Adventures of Huckleberry Finn*:

You don't know about me without you have read a book by the name of *The Adventures of Tom Sawyer*, but that ain't no matter. That book was made by Mr. Mark Twain and he told the truth, mainly. There was things which he stretched, but mainly he told the truth. That is nothing. I never seen anybody but lied one time or another, without it was Aunt Polly or the widow, or maybe Mary. Aunt Polly—Tom's Aunt Polly, she is—and Mary and the Widow Douglas is all told about in that book, which is mostly a true book, with some stretchers as I said before.

Note how much Twain accomplishes in these few sentences, gaining the reader's confidence on behalf of his protagonist and establishing the narrator's voice. It's as though the author were saying, "Lookee here, now, I got a great yarn for you—"

Some sixty-two years after Huck was created, Holden Caulfield appeared in J. D. Salinger's *Catcher in the Rye* and introduced himself to the reader in much the same tone. (It's quoted on page 56.)

Isak Dinesen begins *Out of Africa* with this simple paragraph which sounds as though she were conversing with a friend:

> I had a farm in Africa, at the foot of the Ngong Hills. The Equator runs across these highlands, a hundred miles to the North, and the farm lay at an altitude of over six thousand feet. In the daytime you felt that you had got high up, near to the sun, but the early mornings and evenings were limpid and restful, and the nights were cold.

A subcategory is the teasing beginning wherein the author subtly promises to tell all manner of wonderful things to intrigue the reader into listening to his tale, such as the opening of Jeffry Scott's "The Passing of Mr. Toad":

> The day was idyllic, almost uncannily perfect. That made what followed seem so much worse.

What did happen that day? the reader asks himself, and reads on to find out.

Look what ominous adventures Wilbur Daniel Steele promises with the opening of his story "The Man Who Saw Through Heaven":

> People have wondered (there being no question of romance involved) how I could ever have allowed myself to be let in for the East African adventure of Mrs. Diana in search of her husband. There were several reasons.

My novel, *Matador*, starts out:

It was a very special day, this Sunday in May—

What was the reason? the reader wants to know, and keeps reading.

—not only for Sevilla, the spiritual capital of bullfighting, but for all of the Iberian peninsula and even for many countries in Latin America. People had come from all over Spain and Portugal and many parts of Europe, and what tickets there were left to be scalped by the "revendedores" were going for as high as one hundred and fifty dollars.

11. DIARY, EPISTOLARY, OR REFLECTIVE

In 1740 Samuel Richardson wrote *Pamela or Virtue Rewarded*, a pivotal work in the development of the novel, and it was all told in Pamela's letters to her parents.

Such contemporary works as the long-running play *Love Letters* by A. R. Gurney, *Fair and Tender Ladies* by Lee Smith, *A Woman of Independent Means* by Elizabeth Forsythe Hailey, and the *Griffin & Sabine* trilogy by Nick Bantock are told entirely in letters.

Many stories and novels begin with the device of a character finding a note or receiving a letter that starts with some form of "When you read this I'll be dead (married, gone, living in Tahiti, etc.)."

Josephine Humphreys, in the beginning of her sensitive novel *Rich in Love*, has her young heroine come across a curt note from her mother telling her father that she is leaving him; in a poignant scene the girl rewrites the letter in gentler language so as to soften the blow for her beloved father.

Alice Walker's *The Color Purple* is told in letters and journal style and starts out:

> *You better not never tell nobody but God. It'd kill your mammy.*

Dear God,

I am fourteen years old. I have always been a good girl. Maybe you can give me a sign letting me know what is happening to me.

Last spring after little Lucious come I heard them fussing. He was pulling on her arm. She say It too soon, Fonso, I ain't well. Finally he leave her alone. A week go by, he pulling on her arm again. She say Naw, I ain't gonna. Can't you see I'm already half dead, an all of these chilren.

12. INTERROGATORY

Starting with a question is a fairly common way of starting a story, as in:

> "Jee-zus," he thought as he heard the first strains of *Lohengrin*. "What have I got myself into?"

A question opening is frequently used to begin suspense stories to involve the reader as soon as possible in the action and situation:

> What time was it? Adam looked at his watch for the tenth time. Where were those guys? The dynamite was set to blow in ten minutes and they weren't here! What was keeping them and where was Kate now that he needed her so desperately?

Larry McMurtry starts his novel *Some Can Whistle*, about a writer's long-lost daughter suddenly entering his life, with this question:

"Mister Deck, are you my stinkin' Daddy?" a youthful, female, furious voice said into the phone.

Saul Bellow starts his 1959 novel, *Henderson the Rain King*, thusly:

What made me take this trip to Africa? There is no explanation. Things got worse and worse and worse and pretty soon they were too complicated.

Erich Segal's tear-jerking best-seller of yesteryear, *Love Story*, asked the question:

What can you say about a twenty-five-year-old girl who died?

Anthony Trollope begins his classic novel *Barchester Towers* with the question that constitutes the spine of the rest of his story:

In the latter days of July in the year 185–, a most important question was for ten days hourly asked in the cathedral city of Barchester, and answered every hour in various ways—Who was to be the new Bishop?

So there you have twelve categories of beginnings; you will come up with subheadings of your own and perhaps some beginnings that defy being categorized. But mark this well: The first words of your novel, story, or article may be the most important in terms of readability and salability. Therefore as you sit down to start to write, consider these suggestions and options:

1. Try to pick the most intriguing place in your piece to begin.
2. Try to create attention-grabbing images of a setting if that's where you want to begin.
3. Raise the reader's curiosity about what is happening or is going to happen in an action scene.
4. Describe a character so compellingly that we want to learn more about what happens to him or her.
5. Present a situation so vital to our protagonist that we must read on.
6. And most important, no matter what method you choose, *start with something happening!* (And not with rumination! A character sitting in a cave or in jail or in a kitchen or a car ruminating about the meaning of his or her life and how he or she got to this point does not constitute *something happening.*)

Hone your opening words, for just as stories aren't written but rewritten, so should beginnings be written and rewritten. Look at your opening and ask yourself, "If I were reading this, would I be intrigued enough to go on?"

And remember: Always aim for the heart!

Let's end the chapter with a list, in no order whatsoever, of some well-known beginnings of stories and novels.

In the fall the war was always there, but we did not go to it any more. It was cold in the fall in Milan and the dark came very early.

—Ernest Hemingway
"In Another Country"

The oyster leads a dreadful but exciting life.

> —M. F. K. Fisher
> *Consider the Oyster*

Until I was 8 years I had no thought of getting married. I was seduced on our front lawn and my mother and father were watching.

> —Richard Armour
> *My Life with Women*

In a village of La Mancha the name of which I don't care to recall, there lived not so long ago one of those gentlemen who always have a lance in the rack, an ancient buckler, a skinny nag, and a greyhound for the chase.

> —Miguel de Cervantes
> *Don Quixote*

He—for there could be no doubt of his sex, though the fashion of the time did something to disguise it—was in the act of slicing at the head of a Moor which swung from the rafters.

> —Virginia Woolf
> *Orlando*

While the present century was in its teens, and on one sunshiny morning in June, there drove up to the great iron gate of Miss Pinkerton's academy of young ladies, on Chiswick Mall, a large family coach, with two fat horses in blazing harness, driven by a fat coachman in a three-cornered hat and wig, at the rate of four miles an hour.

> —William Thackeray
> *Vanity Fair*

Amory Blaine inherited from his mother every trait, except the stray inexpressible few, that made him worth while.
—F. Scott Fitzgerald
This Side of Paradise

Alice was beginning to get very tired of sitting by her sister on the bank and of having nothing to do: once or twice she had peeped into the book her sister was reading, but it had no pictures or conversations in it, "and what is the use of a book," thought Alice, "without pictures or conversations?"
—Lewis Carroll
Alice's Adventures in Wonderland

Call me, Ishmael. Feel absolutely free to do so.
—Peter DeVries
The Vale of Laughter

She was so deeply imbedded in my consciousness that for the first year of school I seem to have believed that each of my teachers was my mother in disguise.
—Philip Roth
Portnoy's Complaint

Mother died today.
—Albert Camus
The Stranger

It was to have been a quiet evening at home.
—John D. MacDonald
The Deep Blue Good-by

"To be born again," sang Gibreel Farishta tumbling from the heavens, "first you have to die."
—Salman Rushdie
The Satanic Verses

Nobody could sleep.
>—Norman Mailer
>*The Naked and the Dead*

It was a queer, sultry summer, the summer they electro-cuted the Rosenbergs, and I didn't know what I was doing in New York.
>—Sylvia Plath
>*The Bell Jar*

There once was a boy by the name of Eustace Clarence Scrubb, and he almost deserved it.
>—C. S. Lewis
>*The Voyage of the Dawn Treader*

Cigars had burned low, and we were beginning to sample the disillusionment that usually afflicts old school friends who have met again as men and found themselves with less in common than they had believed they had.
>—James Hilton
>*Lost Horizon*

Died on me finally.
>—Allan Gurganus
>*Oldest Living Confederate Widow Tells All*

For a long time I used to go to bed early.
>—Marcel Proust
>*Swann's Way*

Marley was dead, to begin with.
>—Charles Dickens
>"A Christmas Carol"

"I have been here before," I said; I had been there be-fore; first with Sebastian more than twenty years ago on a cloudless day in June, when the ditches were white with fool's-parsley and meadowsweet and the air heavy with all the scents of summer; it was a day of peculiar splendour, such as our climate affords once or twice a year, when leaf and flower and bird and sun-lit stone and shadow seem all to proclaim the glory of God; and though I had been there so often, in so many moods, it was to that first visit that my heart returned on this, my latest.

—Evelyn Waugh
Brideshead Revisited

Whether I shall turn out to be the hero of my own life, or whether that station will be held by anybody else, these pages must show.

—Charles Dickens
David Copperfield

The cradle rocks above an abyss, and common sense tells us that our existence is but a brief crack of light between two eternities of darkness.

—Vladimir Nabokov
Speak Memory

In the town there were two mutes, and they were always together.

—Carson McCullers
The Heart Is a Lonely Hunter

There were 117 psychoanalysts on the Pan Am flight to Vienna and I'd been treated by at least six of them.

—Erica Jong
Fear of Flying

It was the afternoon of my eighty-first birthday, and I was in bed with my catamite when Ali announced that the archbishop had come to see me.
—Anthony Burgess
Earthly Powers

One dollar and eighty-seven cents. That was all. And sixty cents of it was in pennies.
—O. Henry
"The Gift of the Magi"

I had this story from one who had no business to tell it to me, or to any other. . . .
—Edgar Rice Burroughs
Tarzan of the Apes

Now at last the slowly gathered, long-pent-up fury of the storm broke upon us.
—Winston Churchill
Their Finest Hour

As Gregor Samsa awoke one morning from uneasy dreams he found himself transformed in his bed into a gigantic insect.
—Franz Kafka
"Metamorphosis"

"Tom!"

—Mark Twain
The Adventures of Tom Sawyer

He was born with the gift of laughter and a sense that the world was mad.
—Rafael Sabatini
Scaramouche

I stand at the window of this great house in the south of France as night falls, the night which is leading me to the most terrible morning of my life.

>—James Baldwin
>*Giovanni's Room*

Elmer Gantry was drunk.

>—Sinclair Lewis
>*Elmer Gantry*

Last night I dreamt I went to Manderley again.

>—Daphne du Maurier
>*Rebecca*

Helen Brent had the best-looking legs at the inquest.

>—James Gunn
>*Deadlier Than the Male*

It was the best of times, it was the worst of times.

>—Charles Dickens
>*A Tale of Two Cities*

All children, except one, grow up.

>—James M. Barrie
>*Peter Pan*

There was one thing I want to make clear right off: my baby [age 13] was a virgin the day she met Errol Flynn.

>—Florence Aadland
>*The Big Love*

It was a pleasure to burn.

>—Ray Bradbury
>*Fahrenheit 451*

The past is a foreign country: they do things differently there.

—L. P. Hartley
The Go-Between

The first time I robbed Tiffany's, it was raining.

—John Cheever
Montraldo

Now: start collecting your own favorite beginnings!

CHAPTER TWO

SETTINGS

There are many approaches to the subject of *setting* in novels and short stories—from stingy and economical to gaudy and ostentatious—but the cardinal rule should be:

The setting should contribute to the richness and texture of the story but should never interfere with the flow, the spine, and the thrust of the narrative.

In the old days—I mean the old, *old* days B.T. (Before Television)—one might start a novel with a long and tedious description of, say, a house or the sea or a countryside or the moonlight on the Ganges and perhaps keep the interest of the reader. Take a look at a classic, Thomas Hardy's "The Three Strangers," and see if along about the second or third paragraph you don't find yourself nodding off or at least getting a little glazed of eye:

Among the few features of agricultural England which retain an appearance but little modified by the lapse of centuries, may be reckoned the high, grassy and furzy downs, combs, or ewe-leases, as they are indifferently called, that fill a large area of certain counties in the south and southwest. If any mark of human occupation is met with hereon, it usually takes the form of the solitary cottage of some shepherd.

Fifty years ago such a lonely cottage stood on such a down, and may possibly be standing there now. In spite of its loneliness, however, the spot, by actual measurement, was not more than five miles from a county town. Yet that affected it little. Five miles of irregular upland, during the long inimical seasons, with their sleets, snows, rains, and mists, afford withdrawing space enough to isolate a Timon or a Nebuchadnezzar; much less, in fair weather, to please that less repellent tribe, the poets, philosophers, artists, and others who "conceive and meditate of pleasant things."

Some old earthen camp or barrow, some clump of trees, at least some starved fragment of ancient hedge is usually taken advantage of in the erection of these forlorn dwellings. But, in the present case, such a kind of shelter had been disregarded. Higher Crowstairs, as the house was called, stood quite detached and undefended. The only reason for its precise situation seemed to be the crossing of two footpaths at right angles hard by, which may have crossed thus for five hundred years. Hence the house was exposed on all sides.

But, though the wind up here blew unmistakably when it did blow, and the rain hit hard whenever it fell, the various weathers of the winter season were not quite so formidable on the comb as . . .

See what I mean? *Z-z-z-z*——

This large chunk of description would be off-putting *anywhere* in a story or novel, but these are the important first paragraphs, and it is a *deadly* way to begin a story by today's standards.

Elmore Leonard once was asked, at the Santa Barbara

Writers Conference, how he managed to write such suspense-
ful books. He replied so memorably:

I try to leave out all the parts that readers skip.

The above excerpt from Hardy is a splendid example of the
kind of parts that readers today tend to skip. I don't mean to
be disrespectful of a great writer, and certainly the passage is
atmospheric, but—well, times change, styles change, readers
change.

Now let's look at the beginning of another classic story,
written in 1908, which also features setting. This one is Jack
London's "To Build a Fire," one of the most perfect stories
ever written:

Day had broken cold and gray, exceedingly cold and
gray, when the man turned aside from the main Yukon trail
and climbed the high earthbank, where a dim and little-
travelled trail led eastward through the fat spruce timberland. It was a steep bank, and he paused for breath at the
top, excusing the act to himself by looking at his watch. It
was nine o'clock. There was no sun nor hint of sun, though
there was not a cloud in the sky. It was a clear day, and yet
there seemed an intangible pall over the face of things, a
subtle gloom that made the day dark, and that was due to
the absence of sun. This fact did not worry the man. He
was used to the lack of sun. It had been days since he had
seen the sun, and he knew that a few more days must pass
before that cheerful orb, due south, would just peep above
the sky-line and dip immediately from view.

The man flung a look back along the way he had come.
The Yukon lay a mile wide and hidden under three feet of
ice. On top of this ice were as many feet of snow. It was
all pure white, rolling in gentle undulations where the ice-
jams of the freeze-up had formed. North and south, as far

as his eye could see, it was unbroken white, save for a dark hair-line that curved and twisted from around the spruce-covered island to the south, and that curved and twisted away into the north, where it disappeared behind another spruce-covered island. This dark hair-line was the trail—the main trail—that led south five hundred miles to the Chilcoot Pass, Dyea, and salt water; and that led north seventy miles to Dawson, and still on to the north a thousand miles to Nulato, and finally to St. Michael on Bering Sea, a thousand miles and half a thousand more.

But all this—the mysterious, far-reaching hair-line trail, the absence of sun from the sky, the tremendous cold, and the strangeness and weirdness of it all—made no impression on the man. It was not because he was long used to it. He was a newcomer in the land, a *chechaquo*, and this was his first winter. The trouble with him was that he was without imagination. He was quick and alert in the things of life, but only in the things, and not in the significances. Fifty degrees below zero meant eighty-odd degrees of frost. Such fact impressed him as being cold and uncomfortable, and that was all. It did not lead him to meditate upon his frailty as a creature of temperature, and upon man's frailty in general, able only to live within certain narrow limits of heat and cold; and from there on it did not lead him to the conjectural field of immortality and man's place in the universe. Fifty degrees below zero stood for a bite of frost that hurt and that must be guarded against by the use of mittens, ear-flaps, warm moccasins, and thick socks. Fifty degrees below zero was to him just precisely fifty degrees below zero. That there should be anything more to it than that was a thought that never entered his head.

As he turned to go on, he spat speculatively. There was a sharp, explosive crackle that startled him. He spat again. And again, in the air, before it could fall to the snow, the

spittle crackled. He knew that at fifty below spittle crackled on the snow, but this spittle had crackled in the air. Undoubtedly it was colder than fifty below—how much
colder he did not know.

How alive this writing is! The language is simple, the sentences short and without frill. How we feel the cold! We are
shivering mentally even before the spittle crackles in the air.
But the reason the description of the cold is so effective is because *a man* is placed in this setting and reacts to it. If it were
just a static description with no living creature placed there,
the reader would not become involved.

To write a static description that has no protagonist reacting to it and yet which intrigues the reader takes a rare
kind of genius. Such a one was, of course, Charles Dickens.
In *Bleak House* he does a vigorous number on London fog
such as has never been done before or since:

London. Michaelmas term lately over, and the Lord
Chancellor sitting in Lincoln's Inn Hall. Implacable No-
vember weather. As much mud in the streets as if the waters had but newly retired from the face of the earth, and
it would not be wonderful to meet a Megalosaurus, forty
feet long or so, waddling like an elephantine lizard up
Holborn Hill. Smoke lowering down from chimney-pots,
making a soft black drizzle, with flakes of soot in it as big
as full-grown snowflakes—gone into mourning, one might
imagine, for the death of the sun. Dogs, undistinguishable
in mire. Horses, scarcely better; splashed to their very
blinkers. Foot passengers, jostling one another's umbrellas
in a general infection of ill temper, and losing their foot-
hold at street-corners, where tens of thousands of other
foot passengers have been slipping and sliding since the
day broke (if this day ever broke), adding new deposits to
the crust upon crust of mud, sticking at those points tena-

ciously to the pavement, and accumulating at compound interest.

Fog everywhere. Fog up the river, where it flows among green aits and meadows; fog down the river, where it rolls defiled among the tiers of shipping and the waterside pollutions of a great (and dirty) city. Fog on the Essex marshes, fog on the Kentish heights. Fog creeping into the cabooses of collier-brigs; fog lying out on the yards and hovering in the rigging of great ships; fog drooping on the gunwales of barges and small boats. Fog in the eyes and throats of ancient Greenwich pensioners, wheezing by the firesides of their wards; fog in the stem and bowl of the afternoon pipe of the wrathful skipper, down in his close cabin; fog cruelly pinching the toes and fingers of his shivering little 'prentice boy on deck. Chance people on the bridges peeping over the parapets into a nether sky of fog, with fog all round them, as if they were up in a balloon and hanging in the misty clouds.

Gas looming through the fog in divers places in the streets, much as the sun may, from the spongey fields, be seen to loom by husbandman and ploughboy. Most of the shops lighted two hours before their time—as the gas seems to know, for it has a haggard and unwilling look.

The raw afternoon is rawest, and the dense fog is densest, and the muddy streets are muddiest near that leaden-headed old obstruction, appropriate ornament for the threshold of a leaden-headed old corporation, Temple Bar. And hard by Temple Bar, in Lincoln's Inn Hall, at the very heart of the fog, sits the Lord High Chancellor in his High Court of Chancery.

Never can there come fog too thick, never can there come mud and mire too deep, to assort with the groping and floundering condition which this High Court of Chancery, most pestilent of hoary sinners, holds this day in the sight of heaven and earth.

On such an afternoon, if ever, the Lord High Chancellor ought to be sitting here—as here he is—with a foggy glory round his head, softly fenced in with crimson cloth and curtains, addressed by a large advocate with great whiskers, a little voice, and an interminable brief, and outwardly directing his contemplation to the lantern in the roof, where he can see nothing but fog. On such an afternoon some score of members of the High Court of Chancery bar ought to be—as here they are—mistily engaged in one of the ten thousand stages of an endless cause, tripping one another up on slippery precedents, groping knee-deep in technicalities, running their goat-hair and horsehair warded heads against walls of words and making a pretence of equity with serious faces, as players might. On such an afternoon the various solicitors in the cause, some two or three of whom have inherited it from their fathers, who made a fortune by it, ought to be—as are they not?— ranged in a line, in a long matted well (but you might look in vain for truth at the bottom of it) between the registrar's red table and the silk gowns, with bills, cross-bills, answers, rejoinders, injunctions, affidavits, issues, references to masters, masters' reports, mountains of costly nonsense, piled before them. Well may the court be dim, with wasting candles here and there; well may the fog hang heavy in it, as if it would never get out; well may the stained-glass windows lose their colour and admit no light of day into the place; well may the uninitiated from the streets, who peep in through the glass panes in the door, be deterred from entrance by its owlish aspect and by the drawl, languidly echoing to the roof from the padded dais where the Lord High Chancellor looks into the lantern that has no light in it and where the attendant wigs are all stuck in a fog-bank! This is the Court of Chancery, which has its decaying houses and its blighted lands in every shire, which has its worn-out lunatic in every madhouse and its dead in every churchyard, which has its ruined suitor with his slipshod heels and threadbare dress borrowing and begging through the round of every man's acquaintance, which gives to monied might the means abundantly of wearying out the right, which so exhausts finances, patience, courage, hope, so overthrows the brain and breaks the heart, that there is not an honourable man among its practitioners who would not give—who does not often give—the warning, "Suffer any wrong that can be done you rather than come here!"

This poetic passage, written when Dickens was at the age of forty and at the very height of his great talent, is worth re-reading for its hypnotic rhythms, blazing imagery, and superb language.

But! . . . do something like the above at your own risk!

A great lump of description like that, no matter how well written, is a threat to your narrative thrust no matter where in your novel it appears. (In a short story such an indulgence would be fatal.)

That is because it is mostly

Inert Material!

(Excuse my shouting, but it's important.)

What is inert material? Here is what A. B. Guthrie, author of such exciting novels as *The Big Sky* (and the screenplay for the film *Shane*), says about it in his little book *A Field Guide to Writing Fiction*:

Anything off the story line constitutes what can be called inert material.

Exposition, explanation, description independent of your

running narrative is inert. There it lies, an obstacle to the run of your story, a dam in the current.

And it is so easy to forget or ignore the simple fact that description of an object or process must be integrated with the story's movement.

An inert passage doesn't go anywhere. It exists all by itself, remote from character and action. It is off scene. Take Melville's *Moby-Dick*. Here is page after page of exposition as the author speaks at length of the ship and its components, their appearances and functions. To be sure, all this imparted knowledge comes in useful later on, but nevertheless it lies dead in the living story. It is as if Melville had taken time off from fiction to explain about the ship and its workings. He is preparing the reader for what is to come and being tedious in the process.

Usually, inert material can be activated by the simple expedient of involving a character in the description of the setting, as we saw in the Jack London excerpt.

How well Ambrose Bierce does this right off the bat in his story "A Son of the Gods," establishing mood and tension as well as a sense of place. Nothing inert in this paragraph!

A breezy day and a sunny landscape. An open country to right and left and forward; behind, a wood. In the edge of this wood, facing the open but not venturing into it, long lines of troops, halted. The wood is alive with them, and full of confused noises—the occasional rattle of wheels as a battery of artillery goes into position to cover the advance; the hum and murmur of the soldiers talking; a sound of innumerable feet in the dry leaves that strew the interspaces among the trees; hoarse commands of officers. Detached groups of horsemen are well in front—not altogether exposed—many of them intently watching the crest of a hill a mile away in the direction of the interrupted advance. For this powerful army, moving in battle order through a forest, has met with a formidable obstacle—the open country. The crest of that gentle hill a mile away has a sinister look; it says, Beware! Along it runs a stone wall extending left and right a great distance. Behind the wall is a hedge; behind the hedge are seen the tops of trees in rather straggling order. Among the trees—what? It is necessary to know.

Here are some other examples, starting with W. Somerset Maugham's story "Mayhew":

Capri is a gaunt rock of austere outline, bathed in a deep blue sea; but its vineyards, green and smiling, give it a sort of easy grace. It is friendly, remote and debonair. I find it strange that Mayhew should have settled on this lovely island, for I never knew a man more insensible to beauty. I do not know what he sought there: happiness, freedom, or merely leisure; I know what he found. In this place which appeals so extravagantly to the senses he lived a life entirely of the spirit. For the island is rich with historic associations and over it broods always the enigmatic memory of Tiberius the Emperor.

From his windows which overlooked the Bay of Naples, with the noble shape of Vesuvius changing colour with the changing light, Mayhew saw a hundred places that recalled the Romans and the Greeks. The past began to haunt him. All that he saw for the first time, for he had never been abroad before, excited his fancy; and in his soul stirred the creative imagination.

Notice how quickly Maugham jumps from pure topography to a human being!

We will put up with—may even welcome—some scene setting if we are given a protagonist and the promise of a story to come fairly soon. Look at this example from "The Gold-Bug" by Edgar Allan Poe:

Many years ago, I contracted an intimacy with a Mr. William Legrand. He was of an ancient Huguenot family and had once been wealthy; but a series of misfortunes had reduced him to want. To avoid the mortification consequent upon his disaster, he left New Orleans, the city of his forefathers, and took up his residence at Sullivan's Island, near Charleston, South Carolina.

This island is a very singular one. It consists of little else than the sea sand, and is about three miles long. Its breadth at no point exceeds a quarter of a mile. It is separated from the mainland by a scarcely perceptible creek, oozing its way through a wilderness of reeds and slime, a favorite resort of the marsh hen. The vegetation, as might be supposed, is scant, or at least dwarfish. No trees of any magnitude are to be seen.

Near the western extremity, where Fort Moultrie stands, and where are some miserable frame buildings, tenanted during the summer by the fugitives from Charleston dust and fever, may be found, indeed, the bristly palmetto; but the whole island, with the exception of this western point and a line of hard, white beach on the seacoast, is covered with a dense undergrowth of the sweet myrtle, so much prized by the horticulturists of England. The shrub here often attains the height of fifteen or twenty feet, and forms an almost impenetrable coppice, burthening the air with its fragrance.

In the inmost recess of this coppice, not far from the eastern or more remote end of the island, Legrand had built himself a small hut, which he occupied when I first, by mere accident, made his acquaintance.

In a like manner James Joyce in his story "A Painful Case" names his protagonist and then takes inventory of his surroundings in order to reveal his character:

Mr. James Duffy lived in Chapelizod because he wished to live as far as possible from the city of which he was a citizen and because he found all the other suburbs of Dublin mean, modern and pretentious. He lived in an old sombre house and from his windows he could look into the disused distillery or upwards along the shallow river on which Dublin is built.

The lofty walls of his uncarpeted room were free from pictures. He had himself bought every article of furniture in the room: a black iron bedstead, an iron washstand, four cane chairs, a clothes rack, a coal scuttle, a fender and irons and a square table on which lay a double desk.

A bookcase had been made in an alcove by means of shelves of white wood. The bed was clothed with white bedclothes and a black and scarlet rug covered the foot. A little hand-mirror hung above the washstand and during the day a white-shaded lamp stood as the sole ornament of the mantelpiece.

The books on the white wooden shelves were arranged from below upwards according to bulk. A complete Wordsworth stood at one end of the lowest shelf and a copy of the *Maynooth Catechism*, sewn into the cloth cover of a notebook, stood at one end of the top shelf.

Writing materials were always on the desk. In the desk lay a manuscript translation of Hauptmann's *Michael Kramer*, the stage directions of which were written in purple ink, and a little sheaf of papers held together by a brass pin. In these sheets a sentence was inscribed from time to time, and, in an ironical moment, the headline of an advertisement for Bile Beans had been pasted on to the first sheet.

Granted this inventory is not terribly exciting, but think how boring it would have been had not the author introduced *a person* in the first sentence.

Now I find *this* piece of inventory, lifted from a then-scandalous book-length narrative poem of the twenties, far more lively and revealing of the protagonists than Mr. Joyce's excerpt above. Entitled *The Wild Party*, by Joseph Moncure March, it was a book we kept under our pillows, and I learned the whole poem by heart when I was very young:

> Studio;
> Bedroom;
> Bath;
> Kitchenette:
> Furnished like a third act passion set:
> Oriental;
> Sentimental;
> They owed two months on the rental.
> Pink cushions,
> Blue cushions: overlaid
> With silk: with lace: with gold brocade.
> These lay propped up on a double bed
> That was covered with a Far East tapestry spread.
>
> Chinese dragons with writhing backs:
> Photographs caught to the wall with tacks:
> Their friends in the profession,
> Celebrities for the impression—
> ("So's your old man—Isidore."
> "Faithfully—Ethel Barrymore").
> On a Chinese lacquer tray there stood a
> Gong with tassels, and a brass Buddha.
> Brass candlesticks.
> Orange candles.

An Art vase with broken handles,
Out of which came an upthrusting
Of cherry blossoms that needed dusting.

Books?
Books?
My god! You don't understand.
They were far too busy living first-hand
For books.
Books!

True,
On the table there lay a few
Tattered copies of a magazine,
Confessional;
Professional;
That talked of their friends on the stage and screen.
A Victrola with records
Just went to show
Queenie's Art on the man two floors below.
Being a person of little guile,
He had lent them to her, for just awhile.
Believe it or not—
All this for a smile!
A grand piano stood in the corner
With the air of a coffin waiting for a mourner.

The bath was a horrible give-away.
The floor was dirty:
The towels were grey.
Cups, saucers,
Knives, plates,
Bottles, glasses
In various states
Of vileness, fought for precarious space in
The jumbled world beneath the basin.

The basin top was the temporary home
Of a corkscrew, scissors,
And a brush and comb.
In the basin bowel
Was a Pullman towel
Vividly wrought with red streaks
From Queenie's perfect lips and cheeks.
Behind one faucet, in a stain of rust,
Spattered with talcum powder and dust,
A razor blade had lived for weeks.
Beside it was stuck a cigarette stub.

And the tub?
Oh—never mind the tub!
On the door-knob there hung a pair
Of limp stockings, and a brassiere
Too soiled to wear.

Of the bedroom,
Nothing much to be said.
It had a bureau:
A double bed
With one pillow, and white spread.
Their trunks: boxes.
A chair.
The walls were white and bare.
Only occasional guests slept there:
Queenie and Burrs, preferring air,
Slept with the Chinese dragons instead.

All right, so it's doggerel, but it's great doggerel and wow, do we "see" that apartment and do we learn about its inhabitants from their artifacts. Objects tell us about their owners.

And that should always be uppermost in our minds as we write description of our characters' environments. In fiction, places and things are never as interesting to the readers as human beings, their actions and their reactions; we are less interested in the purple sage than in the riders thereof, less in the architecture of the cathedral than in the hunchback within, less in the river running through it than in the fishermen thereupon, less in the wuthering of the heights than in the amorous doings thereabouts.

I always try to remember Sinclair Lewis's admonition made to me so long ago:

People don't read fiction for information—they read it for emotion.

Of course, you will always have to give some description of the places your fictional characters inhabit in order for us to share their lives. Some surroundings will require more exposition than others; for example, a suburban kitchen will require less description than, say, the site of a Masai initiation rite or a Mount Athos monastery.

But generally the description that immediately involves the protagonist, that most reveals the protagonists' characters and/or furthers the plot, is the most satisfactory and successful.

Let us end the chapter with Hemingway's lovely and deceptively simple opening of *A Farewell to Arms*. For pure description it is hard to beat, and the simple "we lived" promises that this will be a story about people rather than a village or a river or a mountain:

In the late summer of that year we lived in a house in a village that looked across the river and the plain to the mountains. In the bed of the river there were pebbles and boulders, dry and white in the sun, and the water was clear and swiftly moving and blue in the channels. Troops went by the house and down the road and the dust they raised powdered the leaves of the trees. The trunks of the trees

too were dusty and the leaves fell early that year and we
saw the troops marching along the road and the dust rising
and leaves, stirred by the breeze, falling and the soldiers
marching and afterward the road bare and white except for
the leaves.

CHAPTER THREE

CHARACTERIZATION

We all agree that "characters make your story"—

But what methods does a writer employ to show the reader what the characters are like?

Most important (and I shall shout only a few times herein):

> **A protagonist reveals his or her character**
> **by what he does.**
> **Action is character!**

Another way people in stories reveal their characters is by their dialogue or by their thoughts. Or sometimes by both at once. (" 'I love you,' " he said, hoping the nasty slut would die as soon as possible.")

A third very effective way of characterizing is by other characters' behavior toward, and speech to or about, the protagonist.

Still another method is for the author to *tell* the reader directly about a character's personality. ("He was a bad man, a drunk and an arsonist, and all the town knew it.")

If the story is told in the first person, the writer must use various devices to inform the reader of the narrator's character. Thoughts, of course, as well as the observations and opinions of the other members of the cast, are important to the reader's forming an impression of the narrator's persona and physical characteristics.

Mirrors often figure in first-person stories. ("Not a bad build at all," I thought, "for a fifty-year-old former boxer—but maybe a toupee would help.") Though overused, it is a valid way to describe the otherwise "unseen" teller of the tale.

Let us look at some examples of these different ways to characterize.

Edgar Allan Poe writing in the first person in "The Tell-Tale Heart," published in 1843, gives us a vivid picture of a madman's mind in the opening paragraphs. His thoughts reveal his maniacal character as well as relate the events:

True!—nervous—very, very dreadfully nervous I had been and am! but why *will* you say that I am mad? The disease had sharpened my senses—not destroyed—not dulled them. Above all was the sense of hearing acute. I heard all things in the heaven and in the earth. I heard many things in hell. How, then, am I mad? Hearken! and observe how healthily—how calmly I can tell you the whole story.

It is impossible to tell how first the idea entered my brain; but once conceived, it haunted me day and night. Object there was none. Passion there was none. I loved the old man. He had never wronged me. He had never given me insult. For his gold I had no desire. I think it was his eye! Yes, it was this! One of his eyes resembled that of a vulture—a pale blue eye, with a film over it. Whenever it fell upon me, my blood ran cold; and so by degrees—very gradually—I made up my mind to take the life of the old man, and thus rid myself of the eye forever.

Now this is the point. You fancy me mad. Madmen know nothing. But you should have seen *me.* You should have seen how wisely I proceeded—with what caution—with what foresight—with what dissimulation I went to work!

I was never kinder to the old man than during the whole week before I killed him. And every night, about midnight, I turned the latch of his door and opened it—oh, so gently! And then, when I had made an opening sufficient for my head, I put in a dark lantern, all closed, closed, so that no light shone out, and then I thrust in my head. Oh, you would have laughed to see how cunningly I thrust it in! I moved it slowly—very, very slowly, so that I might not disturb the old man's sleep. It took me an hour to place my whole head within the opening so far that I could see him as he lay upon his bed. Ha!—would a madman have been so wise as this? And then, when my head was well in the room, I undid the lantern cautiously—oh, so cautiously— cautiously (for the hinges creaked)—I undid it just so much that a single thin ray fell upon the vulture eye. And this I did for seven long nights—every night just at midnight—but I found the eye always closed; and so it was impossible to do the work; for it was not the old man who vexed me, but his Evil Eye. And every morning, when the day broke, I went boldly into the chamber, and spoke courageously to him, calling him by name in a hearty tone, and inquiring how he had passed the night. So you see he would have been a very profound old man, indeed, to suspect that every night, just at twelve, I looked in upon him while he slept.

Upon the eighth night I was more than usually cautious in opening the door. A watch's minute hand moves more quickly than did mine. Never before that night had I *felt* the extent of my own powers—of my sagacity. I could scarcely contain my feelings of triumph. To think that there I was, opening the door, little by little, and he not even to dream of my secret deeds or thoughts. I fairly chuckled at the idea; and perhaps he heard me; for he moved on the bed suddenly, as if startled. Now you may think that I drew back—but no. His room was as black as pitch with the thick darkness (for the shutters were close fastened, through fear of robbers), and so I knew that he could not see the opening of the door, and I kept pushing it on steadily, steadily.

I had my head in, and was about to open the lantern, when my thumb slipped upon the tin fastening, and the old man sprang up in bed, crying out: "Who's there?"

How much more effective it is for Poe's character to declare immediately that he is sane! It makes him all the crazier as the tension develops and he repeatedly congratulates himself on his cleverness. It is a classic—and chilling—characterization of a psychotic.

Far different are the opening pages of J. D. Salinger's *Catcher in the Rye*, a perennial best-seller since its publication in 1951. Perhaps no one has characterized a rebellious teenager so well in fiction, and he does it in the boy's own words.

If you really want to hear about it, the first thing you'll probably want to know is where I was born, and what my lousy childhood was like, and how my parents were occupied and all before they had me, and all that David Copperfield kind of crap, but I don't feel like going into it, if you want to know the truth.

Every word of Salinger's in the above excerpt tells us something about the boy's attitude, character, background, and circumstances, a model of the narrator's characterizing himself for the reader.

Sherwood Anderson's much-anthologized story "I'm a Fool," written in 1923, is a bittersweet tale of what might

have been. The narrator is a young stableboy who, on his day
off, puts on his best suit and goes to the races. He talks to an
upper-class sister and brother and his girlfriend in the stands
and gives them a successful tip on a horse. In order to
counter his lack of education and money, he makes up a
phony name and wealthy background for them which back-
fires:

There was something else eating at me.

Because Wilbur come back after he had bet the money,
and after that he spent most of his time talking to that Miss
Woodbury, and Lucy Wessen and I was left alone together
like on a desert island. Gee, if I'd only been on the square
or if there had been any way of getting myself on the
square. There ain't any Walter Mathers, like I said to her
and them, and there hasn't ever been one, but if there was,
I bet I'd go to Marietta, Ohio, and shoot him tomorrow.

There I was, big boob that I am. Pretty soon the race
was over, and Wilbur had gone down and collected our
money, and we had a hack downtown, and he stood us a
swell dinner at the West House, and a bottle of champagne
beside.

And I was with that girl and she wasn't saying much,
and I wasn't saying much either. One thing I know. She
wasn't stuck on me because of the lie about my father being rich and all that. There's a way you know. . . . Craps
amighty. There's a kind of girl you see just once in your
life, and if you don't get busy and make hay then you're
gone for good and all and might as well go jump off a
bridge. They give you a look from inside of them somewhere, and it ain't no vamping, and what it means is—you
want that girl to be your wife, and you want nice things
around her like flowers and swell clothes, and you want her
to have the kids you're going to have, and you want good
music played and no ragtime. Gee whizz.

There's a place over near Sandusky, across a kind of bay, and it's called Cedar Point. And when we had had that dinner we went over to it in a launch, all by ourselves. Wilbur and Miss Lucy and that Miss Woodbury had to catch a ten o'clock train back to Tiffin, Ohio, because when you're out with girls like that you can't get careless and miss any trains and stay out all night like you can with some kinds of Janes.

And Wilbur blowed himself to the launch and it cost him fifteen cold plunks, but I wouldn't ever have knew if I hadn't listened. He wasn't no tin horn kind of a sport.

Over at the Cedar Point place we didn't stay around where there was a gang of common kind of cattle at all.

There was big dance halls and dining places for yaps, and there was a beach you could walk along and get where it was dark, and we went there.

She didn't talk hardly at all and neither did I, and I was thinking how glad I was my mother was all right, and always made us kids learn to eat with a fork at table and not swill soup and not be noisy and rough like a gang you see around a race track that way.

Then Wilbur and his girl went away up the beach and Lucy and I set down in a dark place where there was some roots of old trees the water had washed up, and after that, the time, till we had to go back in the launch and they had to catch their trains, wasn't nothing at all. It went like winking your eye.

Here's how it was. The place we were setting in was dark, like I said, and there was the roots from that old stump sticking up like arms, and there was a watery smell, and the night was like—as if you could put your hand out and feel it—so warm and soft and dark and sweet like a orange.

I most cried and I most swore and I most jumped up and danced, I was so mad and happy and sad.

When Wilbur come back from being alone with his girl, and she saw him coming, Lucy she says, "We got to go to the train now," and she was most crying, too, but she never knew nothing I knew, and she couldn't be so all busted up. And then, before Wilbur and Miss Woodbury got up to where she was, she put her face up and kissed me quick and put her head up against me and she was all quivering and—Gee whizz.

Sometimes I hope I have cancer and die. I guess you know what I mean. We went in the launch across the bay to the train like that, and it was dark too. She whispered and said it was like she and I could get out of the boat and walk on the water, and it sounded foolish, but I knew what she meant.

And then quick, we were right at the depot, and there was a big gang of yaps, the kind that goes to the fairs, and crowded and milling around like cattle, and how could I tell her? "It won't be long because you'll write and I'll write to you." That's all she said.

I got a chance like a hay barn afire. A swell chance I got.

And maybe she would write me, down at Marietta that way, and the letter would come back, and stamped on the front of it by the U.S.A. "There ain't any such guy," or something like that, whatever they stamp on a letter that way.

And me trying to pass myself off for a bigbug and a swell—to her, as decent a little body as God ever made. Craps amighty. A swell chance I got.

And then the train come in and she got on, and Wilbur Wessen come and shook hands with me and that Miss Woodbury was nice and bowed to me and I at her and the train went and I busted out and cried like a kid.

Gee. I could have run after that train and made Dan

Patch look like a freight train after a wreck, but socks amighty, what was the use? Did you ever see such a fool?

How well the young man characterizes himself and how we empathize with his poignant loss. As the poet Whittier said:

For of all sad words of tongue or pen,
The saddest are these: "It might have been!"

In a similar vein, Dorothy Parker's "A Telephone Call" characterizes the narrator in a sensitive monologue written in 1928:

Please, God, let him telephone me now. Dear God, let him call me now. I won't ask anything else of You, truly I won't. It isn't very much to ask. It would be so little to You, God, such a little, little thing. Only let him telephone now. Please, God. Please, please, please.

If I didn't think about it, maybe the telephone might ring. Sometimes it does that. If I could think of something else. If I could think of something else. Maybe if I counted five hundred by fives, it might ring by that time. I'll count slowly. I won't cheat. And if it rings when I get to three hundred, I won't stop; I won't answer it until I get to five hundred. Five, ten, fifteen, twenty, twenty-five, thirty, thirty-five, forty, forty-five, fifty. . . . Oh, please ring. Please.

This is the last time I'll look at the clock. I will not look at it again. It's ten minutes past seven. He said he would telephone at five o'clock. "I'll call you at five, darling." I think that's where he said "darling." I'm almost sure he said it there. I know he called me "darling" twice, and the other time was when he said good-bye. "Good-bye, darling." He was busy, and he can't say much in the office, but he called me "darling" twice. He couldn't have minded my calling him up. I know you shouldn't keep telephoning them—I know they don't like that. When you do that, they know you are thinking about them and wanting them, and that makes them hate you. But I hadn't talked to him in three days—not in three days. And all I did was ask him how he was; it was just the way anybody might have called him up. He couldn't have minded that. He couldn't have thought I was bothering him. "No, of course you're not," he said. And he said he'd telephone me. He didn't have to say that. I didn't ask him to, truly I didn't. I'm sure I didn't. I don't think he would say he'd telephone me, and then just never do it. Please don't let him do that, God. Please don't.

"I'll call you at five, darling." "Good-bye, darling." He was busy, and he was in a hurry, and there were people around him, but he called me "darling" twice. That's mine, that's mine. I have that, even if I never see him again. Oh, but that's so little. That isn't enough. Nothing's enough, if I never see him again. Please let me see him again, God. Please, I want him so much. I want him so much. I'll be good, God. I will try to be better. I will, if You will let me see him again. If You will let him telephone me. Oh, let him telephone me now.

Ah, don't let my prayer seem too little to You, God. You sit up there, so white and old, with all the angels about You and the stars slipping by. And I come to You with a prayer about a telephone call. Ah, don't laugh, God. You see, You don't know how it feels. You're so safe, there on Your throne, with the blue swirling under You. Nothing can touch You: no one can twist Your heart in his hands. This is suffering, God, this is bad, bad suffering. Won't you help me? For Your Son's sake, help me. You said You would do whatever was asked of You in His name. Oh, God, in the name of Thine only beloved Son, Jesus Christ, our Lord, let him telephone me now.

Although she is remembered for her sharp wit and funny one-liners, Parker wrote several moving stories, such as "Big Blonde," which focus on character, and she is a master of swift and deep characterizations that arouse wrenching empathy in her reader. Most of her characters, in spite of a surface gloss, ultimately define themselves by their vulnerability.

Now here, for a change of pace, is the beginning of a recent novel, *Story of My Life* by Jay McInerney, in the blunt language of the very young and very angry.

I'm like, I don't believe this shit.

I'm totally pissed at my old man who's somewhere in the Virgin Islands, I don't know where. The check wasn't in the mailbox today which means I can't go to school Monday morning. I'm on the monthly payment program because Dad says wanting to be an actress is some flaky whim and I never stick to anything—this from a guy who's been married five times—and this way if I drop out in the middle of the semester he won't get burned for the full tuition. Meanwhile he buys his new bimbo Tanya who's a year younger than me a 450 SL convertible—always gone for the young ones, haven't we, Dad?—plus her own condo so she can have some privacy to do her writing. Like she can even *read*. He actually believes her when she says she's writing a novel but when I want to spend eight hours a day busting ass at Lee Strasberg it's like, *another one of Alison's crazy ideas*. Story of my life. My old man is fifty-two going on twelve. And then there's Skip Pendleton, which is another reason I'm pissed.

So I'm on the phone screaming at my father's secretary when there's a call on my other line. I go hello and this guy goes, hi, I'm whatever-his-name-is, I'm a friend of Skip's and I say yeah? and he says, I thought maybe we could go out sometime.

And I say, what am I, dial-a-date?

Skip Pendleton's this jerk I was in lust with once for about three minutes. He hasn't called me in like three weeks which is fine, okay, I can deal with that, but suddenly I'm like a baseball card he trades with his friends? Give me a break. So I go to this guy, what makes you think I'd want to go out with you, I don't even know you? and he says, Skip told me about you. Right. So I'm like, what did he tell you? and the guy goes—Skip said you were hot. I say, great, I'm totally honored that the great Skip Pendleton thinks I'm hot. I'm just a jalapeño pepper waiting for some strange burrito, honey. I mean, *really.*

Look how much information we garner or infer about Alison right off the bat in that brief outburst—not just facts about her life but revelations about her character, in and between the lines, as well as about her relationship with other people.

The direct description approach to characterization is favored by some writers, though not for every story.

Here, in his 1926 story, "My Old Man," Hemingway begins with a direct, no-nonsense, head-on description of the father instead of starting with his subject's own words or with the observations of a minor character to characterize him:

I guess looking at it, now, my old man was cut out for a fat guy, one of those regular little roly fat guys you see around, but he sure never got that way, except a little toward the last, and then it wasn't his fault, he was riding over the jumps only and he could afford to carry plenty of weight then. I remember the way he'd pull on a rubber shirt over a couple of jerseys and a big sweat shirt over that, and get me to run with him in the forenoon in the hot sun. He'd have, maybe, taken a trial trip with one of Razzo's skins early in the morning after just getting in from Torino at four o'clock in the morning and beating it out to the stables in a cab and then with the dew all over everything and the sun just starting to get going, I'd help him pull off his boots and he'd get into a pair of sneakers and all these sweaters and we'd start out.

"Come on, kid," he'd say, stepping up and down on his toes in front of the jock's dressing room, "let's get moving."

Dashiell Hammett was famous for creating characters. When John Huston made a famous film of Hammett's 1929 novel, *The Maltese Falcon*, the director literally "shot the book," using virtually all the dialogue and scenes straight from the novel.

This scene occurs in almost the exact middle of the book when private eye Sam Spade meets Caspar Gutman, "the fat man." Both have the same agenda—to find the fabulously valuable black statue of a falcon. Here is a sample of what David Mamet referred to as the "unlimited vocabulary" of aggression:

The fat man moistened his lips with his tongue. "How much is he willing to buy it for?" he asked.

"Ten thousand dollars."

The fat man laughed scornfully. "Ten thousand, and dollars, mind you, not even pounds. That's the Greek for you. Humph! And what did you say to that?"

"I said if I turned it over to him I'd expect the ten thousand."

"Ah, yes, *if*! Nicely put, sir." The fat man's forehead squirmed in a flesh-blurred frown. "They must know," he said only partly aloud, then: "Do they? Do they know what the bird is, sir? What was your impression?"

"I can't help you there," Spade confessed. "There's not much to go by. Cairo didn't say he did and he didn't say he didn't. She said she didn't, but I took it for granted that she was lying."

"That was not an injudicious thing to do," the fat man said, but his mind was obviously not on his words. He scratched his head. He frowned until his forehead was marked by raw red creases. He fidgeted in his chair as much as his size and the size of the chair permitted fidgeting. He shut his eyes, opened them suddenly—wide—and said to Spade: "Maybe they don't." His bulbous pink face slowly lost its worried frown and then, more quickly, took on an expression of ineffable happiness. "If they don't," he cried, and again: "If they don't I'm the only one in the whole wide sweet world who does!"

Spade drew his lips back in a tight smile. "I'm glad I came to the right place," he said.

The fat man smiled too, but somewhat vaguely. Happiness had gone out of his face, though he continued to smile, and caution had come into his eyes. His face was a watchful-eyed smiling mask held up between his thoughts and Spade. His eyes, avoiding Spade's, shifted to the glass at Spade's elbow. His face brightened. "By Gad, sir," he said, "your glass is empty." He got up and went to the table and clattered glasses and siphon and bottle mixing two drinks.

Spade was immobile in his chair until the fat man, with a flourish and a bow and a jocular "Ah, sir, this kind of medicine will never hurt you!" had handed him his refilled glass. Then Spade rose and stood close to the fat man, looking down at him, and Spade's eyes were hard and bright. He raised his glass. His voice was deliberate, challenging: "Here's to plain speaking and clear understanding."

The fat man chuckled and they drank. The fat man sat

down. He held his glass against his belly with both hands and smiled up at Spade. He said: "Well, sir, it's surprising, but it well may be a fact that neither of them does know exactly what that bird is, and that nobody in all this whole wide sweet world knows what it is, saving and excepting only your humble servant, Casper Gutman, Esquire."

"Swell." Spade stood with legs apart, one hand in his trousers-pocket, the other holding his glass. "When you've told me there'll only be two of us who know."

"Mathematically correct, sir"—the fat man's eyes twinkled—"but"—his smile spread—"I don't know for certain that I'm going to tell you."

"Don't be a damned fool," Spade said patiently. "You know what it is. I know where it is. That's why we're here."

"Well, sir, where is it?"

Spade ignored the question.

The fat man bunched his lips, raised his eyebrows, and cocked his head a little to the left. "You see," he said blandly, "I must tell you what I know, but you will not tell me what you know. That is hardly equitable, sir. No, no, I do not think we can do business along those lines."

Spade's face became pale and hard. He spoke rapidly in a low furious voice: "Think again and think fast. I told that punk of yours that you'd have to talk to me before you got through. I'll tell you now that you'll do your talking today or you are through. What are you wasting my time for? You and your lousy secret! Christ! I know exactly what that stuff is that they keep in the subtreasury vaults, but what good does that do me? I can get along without you. God damn you! Maybe you could have got along without me if you'd kept clear of me. You can't now. Not in San Francisco. You'll come in or you'll get out—and you'll do it today."

He turned and with angry heedlessness tossed his glass at the table. The glass struck the wood, burst apart, and splashed its contents and glittering fragments over table and floor. Spade, deaf and blind to the crash, wheeled to confront the fat man again.

The fat man paid no more attention to the glass's fate than Spade did: lips pursed, eyebrows raised, head cocked a little to the left, he had maintained his pink-faced blandness throughout Spade's angry speech, and he maintained it now.

Spade, still furious, said: "And another thing, I don't want—"

The door to Spade's left opened. The boy who had admitted Spade came in. He shut the door, stood in front of it with his hands flat against his flanks, and looked at Spade. The boy's eyes were wide open and dark with wide pupils. Their gaze ran over Spade's body from shoulders to knees, and up again to settle on the handkerchief whose maroon border peeped from the breast-pocket of Spade's brown coat.

"Another thing," Spade repeated, glaring at the boy: "Keep that gunsel away from me while you're making up your mind. I'll kill him. I don't like him. He makes me nervous. I'll kill him the first time he gets in my way. I won't give him an even break. I won't give him a chance. I'll kill him."

The boy's lips twitched in a shadowy smile. He neither raised his eyes nor spoke.

The fat man said tolerantly: "Well, sir, I must say you have a most violent temper."

"Temper?" Spade laughed crazily. He crossed to the chair on which he had dropped his hat, picked up the hat, and set it on his head. He held out a long arm that ended in a thick forefinger pointing at the fat man's belly. His angry voice filled the room. "Think it over and think like hell. You've got till five-thirty to do it in. Then you're either in or out, for keeps." He let his arm drop, scowled at the bland fat man for a moment, scowled at the boy, and went to the door through which he had entered. When he opened the door he turned and said harshly: "Five-thirty—then the curtain."

Notice how Hammett imbues the fat man's every sentence with an underlying odor of larceny. Would *you* buy a used artifact from this man?

Also pay attention to how the author characterizes each speaker at every turn; one needs few of the "he saids" to know exactly who was speaking.

We see in this excerpt what David Mamet maintains:

People may or may not say what they mean—but they always say something designed to get what they want.

Spade and Gutman both want something very badly; and this not only characterizes them, it creates a feeling of tension in the scene as they pussyfoot around each other. Readers *like* tension—readers *like* suspense—which is another way of saying that all successful stories are saturated in conflict.

Even love stories. As someone said:

The most important element in the Romeo and Juliet balcony scene—is the balcony.

The balcony is symbolic of their family feud and the real barrier to their love, hence: conflict.

Somerset Maugham favored the disarmingly direct approach to characterization in many of his countless stories and novels. Here in "The Treasure" he charts a dangerous course: he insists upon telling the reader *everything* about his protagonist's character before the story even begins. Is this the way you would want a story to begin if, say, you were on an airplane en route to Europe? Ultimately, you must be the judge.

Richard Harenger was a happy man. Notwithstanding
what the pessimists, from Ecclesiastes onwards, have said,
this is not so rare a thing to find in this unhappy world, but
Richard Harenger knew it, and that is a very rare thing indeed. The golden mean which the ancients so highly prized
is out of fashion, and those who follow it must put up with
polite derision from those who see no merit in self-restraint
and no virtue in common sense. Richard Harenger shrugged
a polite and amused shoulder. Let others live dangerously,
let others burn with a hard gemlike flame, let others stake
their fortunes on the turn of a card, walk the tightrope that
leads to glory or the grave, or hazard their lives for a
cause, a passion or an adventure. He neither envied the
fame their exploits brought them nor wasted his pity on
them when their efforts ended in disaster.

But it must not be inferred from this that Richard
Harenger was a selfish or a callous man. He was neither.
He was considerate and of a generous disposition. He was
always ready to oblige a friend, and he was sufficiently
well off to be able to indulge himself in the pleasure of
helping others. He had some money of his own, and he occupied in the Home Office a position that brought him an
adequate stipend. The work suited him. It was regular, re-
sponsible and pleasant. Every day when he left the office
he went to his club to play bridge for a couple of hours,
and on Saturdays and Sundays he played golf. He went
abroad for his holidays, staying at good hotels, and visited
churches, galleries and museums. He was a regular first-
nighter. He dined out a good deal. His friends liked him.
He was easy to talk to. He was well read, knowledgeable
and amusing. He was besides of a personable exterior, not
remarkably handsome, but tall, slim and erect of carriage,
with a lean, intelligent face; his hair was growing thin, for
he was now approaching the age of fifty, but his brown
eyes retained their smile and his teeth were all his own. He

had from nature a good constitution, and he had always taken care of himself. There was no reason in the world why he should not be a happy man, and if there had been in him a trace of self-complacency he might have claimed that he deserved to be.

He had the good fortune even to sail safely through those perilous, unquiet straits of marriage in which so many wise and good men have made shipwreck. Married for love in the early twenties, his wife and he, after some years of almost perfect felicity, had drifted gradually apart. Neither of them wished to marry anyone else, so there was no question of divorce (which indeed Richard Harenger's situation in the government service made undesirable), but for convenience' sake, with the help of the family lawyer, they arranged a separation which left them free to lead their lives as each one wished without interference from the other. They parted with mutual expressions of respect and good will.

Richard Harenger sold his house in St. John's Wood and took a flat within convenient walking distance of Whitehall. It had a sitting room which he lined with his books, a dining room into which his Chippendale furniture just fitted, a nice-sized bedroom for himself, and beyond the kitchen a couple of maids' rooms. He brought his cook, whom he had had for many years, from St. John's Wood, but needing no longer so large a staff dismissed the rest of the servants and applied at a registry office for a house-parlourmaid. He knew exactly what he wanted, and he explained his needs to the superintendent of the agency with precision. He wanted a maid who was not too young, first because young women are flighty and secondly because, though he was of mature age and a man of principle, people would talk, the porter and the tradesmen if nobody else, and both for the sake of his own reputation and that of the young person he considered that the applicant should have

reached years of discretion. Besides that he wanted a maid
who could clean silver well. He had always had a fancy for
old silver, and it was reasonable to demand that the forks
and spoons that had been used by a woman of quality
under the reign of Queen Anne should be treated with tenderness and respect. He was of a hospitable nature and
liked to give at least once a week little dinners of not less
than four people and not more than eight. He could trust
his cook to send in a meal that his guests would take pleasure in eating and he desired his parlourmaid to wait with
neatness and dispatch. Then he needed a perfect valet. He
dressed well, in a manner that suited his age and condition,
and he liked his clothes to be properly looked after. The
parlourmaid he was looking for must be able to press trousers and iron a tie, and he was very particular that his
shoes should be well shone. He had small feet, and he took
a good deal of trouble to have well-cut shoes. He had a
large supply, and he insisted that they should be treed up
the moment he took them off. Finally the flat must be kept
clean and tidy. It was of course understood that any applicant for the post must be of irreproachable character, sober,
honest, reliable and of a pleasing exterior. In return for this
he was prepared to offer good wages, reasonable liberty
and ample holidays. The superintendent listened without
batting an eyelash, and telling him that she was quite sure
she could suit him, sent him a string of candidates which
proved that she had not paid the smallest attention to a
word he said. He saw them all personally. Some were obviously inefficient, some looked fast, some were too old,
others too young, some lacked the presence he thought essential; there was not one to whom he was inclined even to
give a trial. He was a kindly, polite man, and he declined
their services with a smile and a pleasant expression of regret. He did not lose patience. He was prepared to inter-

view house-parlourmaids till he found one who was suitable.

Now it is a funny thing about life, if you refuse to accept anything but the best you very often get it: if you utterly decline to make do with what you can get, then somehow or other you are very likely to get what you want. It is as though Fate said, "This man's a perfect fool, he's asking for perfection," and then just out of her feminine wilfulness flung it in his lap. One day the porter of the flats said to Richard Harenger out of a blue sky:

"I hear you're lookin' for a house-parlourmaid, sir. There's someone I know lookin' for a situation as might do."

Now the story has just begun!

Pritchard, the comely house-parlourmaid who is about to be employed by Harenger, will shake up things quite a bit in his smug life. But what a long time Maugham has taken to get going! A modern writer might have started with the porter's statement and then offered indications of Harenger's character and "back story" as the plot progressed.

Now, to illustrate characterization by action and dialogue, one could do no better than to go to that very same Mr. Maugham and his famous short story, "Mr. Know-All." It is not too long and it illustrates so many valuable things so well that we will look at the story in its entirety:

I was prepared to dislike Max Kelada even before I knew him. The war had just finished and the passenger traffic in the ocean-going liners was heavy. Accommodation was very hard to get and you had to put up with whatever the agents chose to offer you. You could not hope for a cabin to yourself and I was thankful to be given one in which there were only two berths. But when I was told the name of my companion my heart sank. It suggested closed port-holes and the night air rigidly excluded. It was bad enough to share a cabin for fourteen days with anyone (I was going from San Francisco to Yokohama), but I should have looked upon it with less dismay if my fellow-passenger's name had been Smith or Brown.

When I went on board I found Mr Kelada's luggage already below. I did not like the look of it; there were too many labels on the suitcases, and the wardrobe trunk was too big. He had unpacked his toilet things, and I observed that he was a patron of the excellent Monsieur Coty; for I saw on the washing-stand his scent, his hair-wash, and his brilliantine. Mr Kelada's brushes, ebony with his monogram in gold, would have been all the better for a scrub. I did not at all like Mr Kelada. I made my way into the smoking-room. I called for a pack of cards and began to play patience. I had scarcely started before a man came up to me and asked me if he was right in thinking my name was so-and-so.

"I am Mr Kelada," he added, with a smile that showed a row of flashing teeth, and sat down.

"Oh, yes, we're sharing a cabin, I think."

"Bit of luck, I call it. You never know who you're going to be put in with. I was jolly glad when I heard you were English. I'm all for us English sticking together when we're abroad, if you understand what I mean."

I blinked.

"Are you English?" I asked, perhaps tactlessly.

"Rather. You don't think I look an American, do you? British to the backbone, that's what I am."

To prove it, Mr Kelada took out of his pocket a passport and airily waved it under my nose.

King George has many strange subjects. Mr Kelada was short and of a sturdy build, clean-shaven and dark-skinned, with a fleshy, hooked nose and very large, lustrous and liquid eyes. His long black hair was sleek and curly. He spoke with a fluency in which there was nothing English and his gestures were exuberant. I felt pretty sure that a closer inspection of that British passport would have betrayed the fact that Mr Kelada was born under a bluer sky than is generally seen in England.

"What will you have?" he asked me.

I looked at him doubtfully. Prohibition was in force and to all appearances the ship was bone-dry. When I am not thirsty I do not know which I dislike more, ginger-ale or lemon-squash. But Mr Kelada flashed an oriental smile at me.

"Whisky and soda or a dry Martini, you have only to say the word."

From each of his hip-pockets he fished a flask and laid them on the table before me. I chose the Martini, and calling the steward he ordered a tumbler of ice and a couple of glasses.

"A very good cocktail," I said.

"Well, there are plenty more where that came from, and if you've got any friends on board, you tell them you've got a pal who's got all the liquor in the world."

Mr Kelada was chatty. He talked of New York and of San Francisco. He discussed plays, pictures, and politics. He was patriotic. The Union Jack is an impressive piece of drapery, but when it is flourished by a gentleman from Alexandria or Beirut, I cannot but feel that it loses somewhat in dignity. Mr Kelada was familiar. I do not wish to put on airs, but I cannot help feeling that it is seemly in a total stranger to put mister before my name when he addresses me. Mr Kelada, doubtless to set me at my ease, used no such formality. I did not like Mr Kelada. I had put aside the cards when he sat down, but now, thinking that for this first occasion our conversation had lasted long enough, I went on with my game.

"The three on the four," said Mr Kelada.

There is nothing more exasperating when you are playing patience than to be told where to put the card you have turned up before you have had a chance to look for yourself.

"It's coming out, it's coming out," he cried. "The ten on the knave."

With rage and hatred in my heart I finished. Then he seized the pack.

"Do you like card tricks?"

"No, I hate card tricks," I answered.

"Well, I'll just show you this one."

He showed me three. Then I said I would go down to the dining-room and get my seat at table.

"Oh, that's all right," he said. "I've already taken a seat for you. I thought that as we were in the same state-room we might just as well sit at the same table."

I did not like Mr Kelada.

I not only shared a cabin with him and ate three meals a day at the same table, but I could not walk round the deck without his joining me. It was impossible to snub him. It never occurred to him that he was not wanted. He was certain that you were as glad to see him as he was to see you. In your own house you might have kicked him downstairs and slammed the door in his face without the suspicion dawning on him that he was not a welcome visitor. He was a good mixer, and in three days knew everyone on board. He ran everything. He managed the sweeps, conducted the auctions, collected money for prizes at the sports, got up quoit and golf matches, organized the concert, and arranged the fancy-dress ball. He was everywhere and always. He was certainly the best-hated man in the ship. We called him Mr Know-All, even to his face. He took it as a compliment. But it was at meal times that he was most intolerable. For the better part of an hour then he had us at his mercy. He was hearty, jovial, loquacious and argumentative. He knew everything better than anybody else, and it was an affront to his overweening vanity that you should disagree with him. He would not drop a subject, however unimportant, till he had brought you round to his way of thinking. The possibility that he could be mistaken never occurred to him. He was the chap who knew. We sat at the doctor's table. Mr Kelada would certainly have had it all his own way, for the doctor was lazy and I was frigidly indifferent, except for a man called Ramsay who sat there also. He was as dogmatic as Mr Kelada and resented bitterly the Levantine's cocksureness. The discussions they had were acrimonious and interminable.

Ramsay was in the American Consular Service, and was stationed at Kobe. He was a great heavy fellow from the Middle West, with loose fat under a tight skin, and he bulged out of his ready-made clothes. He was on his way back to resume his post, having been on a flying visit to New York to fetch his wife, who had been spending a year at home. Mrs Ramsay was a very pretty little thing, with pleasant manners and a sense of humour. The Consular Service is ill paid, and she was dressed always very simply; but she knew how to wear her clothes. She achieved an effect of quiet distinction. I should not have paid any particular attention to her but that she possessed a quality that may be common enough in women, but nowadays is not obvious in their demeanour. You could not look at her without being struck by her modesty. It shone in her like a flower on a coat.

One evening at dinner the conversation by chance drifted to the subject of pearls. There had been in the papers a good deal of talk about the culture pearls which the cunning Japanese were making, and the doctor remarked that they must inevitably diminish the value of real ones. They were very good already; they would soon be perfect. Mr Kelada, as was his habit, rushed the new topic. He told us all that was to be known about pearls. I do not believe Ramsay knew anything about them at all, but he could not resist the opportunity to have a fling at the Levantine, and in five minutes we were in the middle of a heated argument. I had seen Mr Kelada vehement and voluble before, but never so voluble and vehement as now. At last something that Ramsay said stung him, for he thumped the table and shouted:

"Well, I ought to know what I am talking about. I'm going to Japan just to look into this Japanese pearl business. I'm in the trade and there's not a man in it who won't tell you that what I say about pearls goes. I know all the best pearls in the world, and what I don't know about pearls isn't worth knowing."

Here was news for us, for Mr Kelada, with all his loquacity, had never told anyone what his business was. We only knew vaguely that he was going to Japan on some commercial errand. He looked round the table triumphantly.

"They'll never be able to get a culture pearl that an expert like me can't tell with half an eye." He pointed to a chain that Mrs Ramsay wore. "You take my word for it, Mrs Ramsay, that chain you're wearing will never be worth a cent less than it is now."

Mrs Ramsay in her modest way flushed a little and slipped the chain inside her dress. Ramsay leaned forward. He gave us all a look and a smile flickered in his eyes.

"That's a pretty chain of Mrs Ramsay's, isn't it?"

"I noticed it at once," answered Mr Kelada. "Gee, I said to myself, those are pearls all right."

"I didn't buy it myself, of course. I'd be interested to know how much you think it cost."

"Oh, in the trade somewhere round fifteen thousand dollars. But if it was bought on Fifth Avenue I shouldn't be surprised to hear that anything up to thirty thousand was paid for it."

Ramsay smiled grimly.

"You'll be surprised to hear that Mrs Ramsay bought that string at a department store the day before we left New York, for eighteen dollars."

Mr Kelada flushed.

"Rot. It's not only real, but it's as fine a string for its size as I've ever seen."

"Will you bet on it? I'll bet you a hundred dollars it's imitation."

"Done."

"Oh, Elmer, you can't bet on a certainty," said Mrs Ramsay.

She had a little smile on her lips and her tone was gently deprecating.

"Can't I? If I get a chance of easy money like that I should be all sorts of a fool not to take it."

"But how can it be proved?" she continued. "It's only my word against Mr Kelada's."

"Let me look at the chain, and if it's imitation I'll tell you quickly enough. I can afford to lose a hundred dollars," said Mr Kelada.

"Take it off, dear. Let the gentleman look at it as much as he wants."

Mrs Ramsay hesitated a moment. She put her hands to the clasp.

"I can't undo it," she said. "Mr Kelada will just have to take my word for it."

I had a sudden suspicion that something unfortunate was about to occur, but I could think of nothing to say.

Ramsay jumped up.

"I'll undo it."

He handed the chain to Mr Kelada. The Levantine took

a magnifying glass from his pocket and closely examined it. A smile of triumph spread over his smooth and swarthy face. He handed back the chain. He was about to speak. Suddenly he caught sight of Mrs Ramsay's face. It was so white that she looked as though she were about to faint. She was staring at him with wide and terrified eyes. They held a desperate appeal; it was so clear that I wondered why her husband did not see it.

Mr Kelada stopped with his mouth open. He flushed deeply. You could almost *see* the effort he was making over himself.

"I was mistaken," he said. "It's a very good imitation, but of course as soon as I looked through my glass I saw that it wasn't real. I think eighteen dollars is just about as much as the damned thing's worth."

He took out his pocket-book and from it a hundred-dollar note. He handed it to Ramsay without a word.

"Perhaps that'll teach you not to be so cocksure another time, my young friend," said Ramsay as he took the note.

I noticed that Mr Kelada's hands were trembling.

The story spread over the ship as stories do, and he had to put up with a good deal of chaff that evening. It was a fine joke that Mr Know-All had been caught out. But Mrs Ramsay retired to her state-room with a headache.

Next morning I got up and began to shave. Mr Kelada lay on his bed smoking a cigarette. Suddenly there was a small scraping sound and I saw a letter pushed under the door. I opened the door and looked out. There was nobody there. I picked up the letter and saw that it was addressed to Max Kelada. The name was written in block letters. I handed it to him.

"Who's this from?" He opened it. "Oh!"

He took out of the envelope, not a letter, but a hundred-dollar note. He looked at me and again he reddened. He tore the envelope into little bits and gave them to me.

"Do you mind just throwing them out of the port-hole?"

I did as he asked, and then I looked at him with a smile.

"No one likes being made to look a perfect damned fool," he said.

"Were the pearls real?"

"If I had a pretty little wife I shouldn't let her spend a year in New York while I stayed at Kobe," said he.

At that moment I did not entirely dislike Mr Kelada. He reached out for his pocket-book and carefully put in it the hundred-dollar note.

So there you have a perfect little story of its genre. It does to perfection what its author sets out to do—and all based on characters; in lesser hands it would be but an anecdote.

Have we not all met someone like Mr. Kelada?

F. Scott Fitzgerald wrote:

Begin with an individual, and before you know it you find you have created a type; begin with a type, and you find you have created—nothing.

Mr. Kelada is an individual—we have not met anyone *exactly* like him before in literature—yet he is also a type.

How very well we get to know him—and dislike him—*by his actions* and *his dialogue*. The narrator *tells* us that he doesn't like Max but then successfully *shows* us the man's boorishness over and over to prove why he doesn't like him. He even points out the man's dirty hairbrushes.

When the narrator says he hates card tricks, Max blithely goes ahead and does three for him. His pushiness knows no limits.

But Maugham does not stint with the characterizations of the other two people in the story, Mr. and Mrs. Ramsay; though they are not as detailed, we see them very clearly.

When analyzing the components of stories, people often cite "The Four Vital C's":

Characters, Conflict, Choice, and Change

(Sometimes "Compassion" or "Caring" is added.) This little story of Maugham's has all those elements.

Character is emphasized at every turn. *Conflict* is present from the very first sentence. *Choice* was clearly made by Max—a humiliating and devastating choice for a man of his egocentric character. And a *Change* in how both the readers and the narrator regard Max at the end is obvious. As for *Compassion* or *Caring*, Maugham, often regarded as a cynic, had an abundance of that for the characters that peopled his creations, whether heroes, antiheroes, or villains.

Some tips on how to characterize:

Make a list of the characters in your story and opposite their names state what they want, for example:

Mark, 18—wants to find out who his real father is.

Jane, 38—never wants the truth to come out, that the man she married is in prison for murder. She wants silence at any cost.

Bill, 42—knows who the real killer is, wants only to marry Jane.

If your characters do not *want* anything, they will be lifeless and boring.

Once Ray Bradbury told me the simplest and best suggestion for plotting:

Find out what your hero or heroine wants, and when he or she wakes up in the morning, just follow him or her all day.

Sol Stein, one of the most popular teachers at the Santa Barbara Writers Conference, writes in his book *Stein on Writing*:

> Inexperienced writers, sometimes ill-read in the great works of their own and previous times, often try to write novels with a relatively passive protagonist who wants little or has largely given up wanting. I have met more than one writer who says that his character doesn't want anything— he just wants to "live his life."

That brings to mind something Kurt Vonnegut once said:

> When I used to teach creative writing, I would tell the students to make their characters want something right away even if it's only a glass of water. Characters paralyzed by the meaninglessness of modern life still have to drink water from time to time.

The most interesting stories involve characters who want something badly. In Kafka's *Trial*, Josef K. wants to know why he is being arrested, why he is being tried, what he is guilty of. In Scott Fitzgerald's *Great Gatsby*, the central character constructs his life with the sole object of reuniting with Daisy, the woman he loves. In Flaubert's *Madame Bovary*, Emma Bovary, her head full of romantic notions, wants to escape the dreariness of her husband and life. If your character doesn't want anything badly enough, readers will have a hard time rooting for him to attain his goal, which is what compels readers to continue reading. The more urgent the want, the greater the reader's interest. A far-future want does not set the reader's pulse going the way an immediate want does. The want can be negative— wanting something *not* to happen—as in Frederick Forsyth's *Day of the Jackal*, in which the reader hopes that de Gaulle will escape the assassin's bullet.

If you are having trouble locating the core of a character, ask yourself:

> How would he or she behave in a quarrel? (Write a scene where the character has a serious argument with another character.)
> What kind of a letter would your character write?
> What would your character say in a suicide note? Write it out!

Fill out a mythical questionnaire for your character: place of birth, age of parents at their death, pets as a child, schooling, military service if any, first loves, marriage, relationship with children, and so on.

Sinclair Lewis told me that he often wrote a 10,000-word biography for each of the principals before starting a new novel. He might end up using little of that material in the final work, but the process gave him insights into his characters he would not otherwise have had.

We rarely remember the convolutions of the plots of great books like *War and Peace*, *David Copperfield*, *Gone with the Wind*, and *Roots*—but we remember Pierre, Mr. Micawber, Scarlett, and Kizzy as though they were members of our families.

The authors of those books understood so well that

Characters make your story!

CHAPTER FOUR

INDIVIDUALIZING

Individualizing is a most important part of characterization, but they are not the same thing and should not be confused.

What is the difference?

When, as a fledgling writer, I asked Sinclair Lewis what the difference was, he replied:

Let's say your protagonist is a legless man coming down the street propelling himself along on one of those little platforms with wheels. That is *individualizing* your character in the extreme—how many stories have legless men as main characters? But you have not characterized him yet—he must do that by his speech and/or his actions. For example, if in passing a blind man, he fumbles into his threadbare shirt, finds a quarter, his last quarter, says "God bless you," and gives it to the man, he is characterized as well as individualized. If, instead, he curses the blind man, reaches up and steals his pencils and whacks the seeing eye dog on the nose, he is characterized as another type of person.

(And my guess is that if Sinclair Lewis were to write that scene he couldn't resist having the blind man take off his dark glasses and clobber the bad guy.)

Characterizing and individualizing often go hand in hand which, of course, is to be desired. *Little Women*, Louisa May Alcott's 1869 novel, one of the most enduring books ever written, owes its enormous popularity to its varied, vivid, endearing portraits of the four individual sisters and their mother. On the very first page the author characterizes and begins to individualize the girls:

"Christmas won't be Christmas without any presents," grumbled Jo, lying on the rug.

"It's so dreadful to be poor!" sighed Meg, looking down at her old dress.

"I don't think it's fair for some girls to have plenty of pretty things, and other girls nothing at all," added little Amy, with an injured sniff.

"We've got father and mother and each other," said Beth contentedly, from her corner.

The four young faces on which the firelight shone brightened at the cheerful words, but darkened again as Jo said sadly:

"We haven't got father, and shall not have him for a long time." She didn't say "perhaps never," but each silently added it, thinking of father far away, where the fighting was.

Nobody spoke for a minute; then Meg said in an altered tone:

"You know the reason mother proposed not having any presents this Christmas was because it is going to be a hard winter for everyone; and she thinks we ought not to spend money for pleasure, when our men are suffering so in the army. We can't do much, but we can make our little sacrifices, and ought to do it gladly. But I am afraid I don't";

and Meg shook her head as she thought regretfully of all the pretty things she wanted.

"But I don't think the little we should spend would do any good. We've each got a dollar, and the army wouldn't be much helped by our giving that. I agree not to expect anything from mother or you, but I do want to buy 'Undine and Sintram' for myself; I've wanted it *so* long," said Jo, who was a bookworm.

"I have planned to spend mine in new music," said Beth, with a little sigh, which no one heard but the hearth brush and kettle holder.

"I shall get a nice box of Faber's drawing pencils; I really need them," said Amy decidedly.

"Mother didn't say anything about our money, and she won't wish us to give up everything. Let's each buy what we want, and have a little fun; I'm sure we work hard enough to earn it," cried Jo, examining the heels of her shoes in a gentlemanly manner.

"I know *I* do—teaching those tiresome children nearly all day, when I'm longing to enjoy myself at home," began Meg, in the complaining tone again.

"You don't have half such a hard time as I do," said Jo. "How would you like to be shut up for hours with a nervous, fussy old lady, who keeps you trotting, is never satisfied, and worries you till you're ready to fly out of the window or cry?"

"It's naughty to fret; but I do think washing dishes and keeping things tidy is the worst work in the world. It makes me cross; and my hands get so stiff, I can't practice well at all"; and Beth looked at her rough hands with a sigh that anyone could hear that time.

"I don't believe any of you suffer as I do," cried Amy; "for you don't have to go to school with impertinent girls, who plague you if you don't know your lessons, and laugh at your dresses, and label your father if he isn't rich, and insult you when your nose isn't nice."

"If you mean *libel*, I'd say so, and not talk about *labels*, as if papa was a pickle bottle," advised Jo, laughing.

"I know what I mean, and you needn't be *statirical* about it. It's proper to use good words, and improve your *vocabilary*," returned Amy, with dignity.

By their talk shall we know them!

Alcott realized how important dialogue can be to individualizing the people in her story as well as revealing their characters; in two pages we have come to know, at least superficially, four very different girls.

Also notice how, though we have not even yet seen the mother, we learn quite a bit about her character from the girls' talk and attitude. Notice also how much we learn about the family and their activities from this brief excerpt. Whether or not *Little Women* is considered great literature or well written, it has been a lasting pleasure for generations of readers. As Somerset Maugham has written:

> *If you can tell stories, create characters, devise incidents, and have sincerity and passion, it doesn't matter a damn how well you write.*

Eudora Welty has said, in her little book *One Writer's Beginnings*, that she does not try for specific portraits of real people in her novels, that she invents them along with the story. But—and this is a large *but*—

> Attached to them are what I've borrowed, perhaps unconsciously, bit by bit, of persons I have seen or noticed or remembered in the flesh—a cast of countenance here, a manner of walking there, that jump to the visualizing mind when a story is underway. (Elizabeth Bowen said, "Physical

detail cannot be invented." It can only be chosen.) I don't write by invasion into the life of a real person; my own sense of privacy is too strong for that; and I also know instinctively that living people to whom you are close—those known to you in ways too deep, too overflowing, ever to be plumbed outside love—do not yield to, could never fit into, the demands of a story. On the other hand, what I do make my stories out of is the *whole* fund of my feelings, my responses to the real experiences of my own life, to the relationships that formed and changed it, that I have given most of myself to, and so learned my way toward a dramatic counterpart. Characters take on life sometimes by luck, but I suspect it is when you can write most entirely out of yourself, inside the skin, heart, mind, and soul of a person who is not yourself, that a character becomes in his own right another human being on the page.

And this is, of course, what makes Miss Welty's characters so memorable and like no others we have met in literature. Her characters are *round*, as opposed to *flat*.

How do you tell the difference between a round character and a flat one?

E. M. Forster said:

The test of a round character is whether it is capable of surprising in a convincing way. If it never surprises, it is flat.

As novelist-biographer John Leggett tells his classes at the Santa Barbara Writers Conference:

In fiction of quality, the protagonist is likely to be a *round* character. A round character is fleshed out with a great many different traits and qualities. Though the round character may be the central player, flat characters are sometimes necessary to get the best of stories told.

It is the mark of a classic short story that there be but one major character, so complexity will be properly lavished there. Supporting characters had better be kept simple to prevent their stealing the story's focus.

We readers have a limited capacity for meeting new characters and sorting them out. Nothing is more daunting than confronting, early on in a story, a crowd of strangers without a proper introduction. It is worse if their names are similar. To assimilate a character we need a portrait or a situation which stamps that character in our memory.

Vladimir Nabokov created several unforgettable, round characters in his 1958 novel, *Lolita*. The story of an older man's obsessive love for a young girl, it was considered scandalous at the time, but has become something of a classic. The book heralded Nabokov as one of the great language stylists of modern times.

In this excerpt Mr. Humbert Humbert is traveling around America, motel after motel, with the eponymous heroine; and while Nabokov gives us a European's look at this slice of Americana, he never forgets to *individualize* and *characterize* "Lo" at every opportunity. While he never forgets that she is a child, she is of a very different stripe than the little women of Louisa May Alcott's March family:

A combination of naïveté and deception, of charm and vulgarity, of blue sulks and rosy mirth, Lolita, when she chose, could be a most exasperating brat. I was not really quite prepared for her fits of disorganized boredom, intense and vehement griping, her sprawling, droopy, dopey-eyed style, and what is called goofing off—a kind of diffused clowning which she thought was tough in a boyish hoodlum way. Mentally, I found her to be a disgustingly conventional little girl. Sweet hot jazz, square dancing, gooey fudge sundaes, musicals, movie magazines and so forth—these were the obvious items in her list of beloved things. The Lord knows how many nickels I fed to the gorgeous music boxes that came with every meal we had! I still hear the nasal voices of those invisibles serenading her, people with names like Sammy and Jo and Eddy and Tony and Peggy and Guy and Patty and Rex, and sentimental song hits, all of them as similar to my ears as her various candies were to my palate. She believed, with a kind of celestial trust, any advertisement or advice that appeared in *Movie Love* or *Screen Land*—Starasil Starves Pimples, or "You better watch out if you're wearing your shirttails outside your jeans, gals, because Jill says you shouldn't." If a roadside sign said: VISIT OUR GIFT SHOP—we *had* to visit it, *had* to buy its Indian curios, dolls, copper jewelry, cactus candy. The words "novelties and souvenirs" simply entranced her by their trochaic lilt. If some café sign proclaimed Icecold Drinks, she was automatically stirred, although all drinks everywhere were ice-cold. She it was to whom ads were dedicated: the ideal consumer, the subject and object of every foul poster. And she attempted—unsuccessfully—to patronize only those restaurants where the holy spirit of Huncan Dines had descended upon the cute paper napkins and cottage-cheese-crested salads. . . .

Every morning during our yearlong travels I had to devise some expectation, some special point in space and time for her to look forward to, for her to survive till bedtime. Otherwise, deprived of a shaping and sustaining purpose, the skeleton of her day sagged and collapsed. The object in view might be anything—a lighthouse in Virginia, a natural cave in Arkansas converted to a café, a collection of guns and violins somewhere in Oklahoma, a replica of the Grotto of Lourdes in Louisiana, shabby photographs of the bonanza mining period in the local museum of a Rocky

Mountain resort, anything whatsoever—but it had to be there, in front of us, like a fixed star, although as likely as not Lo would feign gagging as soon as we got to it.

Have we all not met a child with a bit of Lolita in her? One can see what Fitzgerald meant when he said that when a writer begins with an individual, he probably will end up with a type. Fitzgerald himself always created individuals in his stories and novels. Witness our brief but intriguing first meeting with Mr. Jay Gatsby, the eponymous protagonist of Fitzgerald's classic novel:

I turned again to my new acquaintance. "This is an unusual party for me. I haven't even seen the host. I live over there—" I waved my hand at the invisible hedge in the distance, "and this man Gatsby sent over his chauffeur with an invitation."

For a moment he looked at me as if he failed to understand.

"I'm Gatsby," he said suddenly.

"What!" I exclaimed. "Oh, I beg your pardon."

"I thought you knew, old sport. I'm afraid I'm not a very good host."

He smiled understandingly—much more than understandingly. It was one of those rare smiles with a quality of eternal reassurance in it, that you may come across four or five times in life. It faced—or seemed to face—the whole eternal world for an instant, and then concentrated on *you* with an irresistible prejudice in your favor. It understood you just as far as you wanted to be understood, believed in you as you would like to believe in yourself, and assured you that it had precisely the impression of you that, at your best, you hoped to convey. Precisely at that point it vanished—and I was looking at an elegant young roughneck, a year or two over thirty, whose elaborate formality of speech just missed being absurd. Some time before he introduced himself I'd got a strong impression that he was picking his words with care.

Almost at the moment when Mr. Gatsby identified himself, a butler hurried toward him with the information that Chicago was calling him on the wire. He excused himself with a small bow that included each of us in turn.

In *The Great Gatsby*, we see the protagonist through the narrator's eyes. In *The Silence of the Lambs*, Thomas Harris doesn't directly characterize or individualize Clarice Starling, a fledgling FBI agent; he lets another character do it, which is more effective than having the author's voice intrude. Harris has the brilliant serial murderer Dr. Lecter (who was also in *Red Dragon*), one of the more sinister and individualized villains in modern literature, size up the young woman from his maximum security cell:

When he spoke again, his tone was soft and pleasant. "You'd like to quantify me, Officer Starling. You're so ambitious, aren't you? Do you know what you look like to me, with your good bag and your cheap shoes? You look like a rube. You're a well-scrubbed, hustling rube with a little taste. Your eyes are like cheap birthstones—all surface shine when you stalk some little answer. And you're bright behind them, aren't you? Desperate not to be like your mother. Good nutrition has given you some length of bone, but you're not more than one generation out of the mines, *Officer* Starling. Is it the West Virginia Starlings or the Okie Starlings, Officer? It was a toss-up between college and the opportunities in the Women's Army Corps, wasn't it? Let me tell you something specific about yourself, Student Starling . . ."

We see and get to know our heroine so well in this one paragraph. How much more convincing this method is than if the author himself had ticked off a list of Clarice's characteristics and background information.

Never fail to use one character to characterize another.

Homer knew the value of characterizing by other characters. In the *Iliad* the soldiers are grumbling about the war after being in Troy ten long years. They want to go back home to Greece. This is the only war in history where both sides knew exactly what they were fighting for—Helen of Troy—but the soldiers are battle-weary and homesick. Then radiant Helen walks by. "Did you see *that*!?" The men stare at her unbelievable beauty, then grab their weapons enthusiastically, and charge back into the fight, home and wife forgotten.

Now, one does not have to have an enigmatic or glamorous figure like Gatsby or Hannibal Lecter or Lolita to characterize or individualize. In the hands of a skilled writer even a seemingly dull character like Evan Connell's Mrs. Bridge becomes alive, individualized, and important to us. Similarly, Flannery O'Connor describes two seemingly very ordinary people in her short story "Everything That Rises Must Converge." Here's how it begins:

She was almost ready to go, standing before the hall mirror, putting on her hat, while he, his hands behind him, appeared pinned to the door frame, waiting like Saint Sebastian for the arrows to begin piercing him. The hat was new and had cost her seven dollars and a half. She kept saying, "Maybe I shouldn't have paid that for it. No, I shouldn't have. I'll take it off and return it tomorrow. I shouldn't have bought it."

Julian raised his eyes to heaven. "Yes, you should have

bought it," he said. "Put it on and let's go." It was a hideous hat. A purple velvet flap came down on one side of it and stood up on the other; the rest of it was green and looked like a cushion with the stuffing out. He decided it was less comical than jaunty and pathetic. Everything that gave her pleasure was small and depressed him.

She lifted the hat one more time and set it down slowly on top of her head. Two wings of gray hair protruded on either side of her florid face, but her eyes, sky-blue, were as innocent and untouched by experience as they must have been when she was ten. Were it not that she was a widow who had struggled fiercely to feed and clothe and put him through school and who was supporting him still, "until he got on his feet," she might have been a little girl that he had to take to town.

"It's all right, it's all right," he said. "Let's go." He opened the door himself and started down the walk to get her going. The sky was a dying violet and the houses stood out darkly against it, bulbous liver-colored monstrosities of a uniform ugliness though no two were alike. Since this had been a fashionable neighborhood forty years ago, his mother persisted in thinking they did well to have an apartment in it. Each house had a narrow collar of dirt around it in which sat, usually, a grubby child. Julian walked with his hands in his pockets, his head down and thrust forward and his eyes glazed with the determination to make himself completely numb during the time he would be sacrificed to her pleasure.

The door closed and he turned to find the dumpy figure, surmounted by the atrocious hat, coming toward him. "Well," she said, "you only live once and paying a little more for it, I at least won't meet myself coming and going."

"Some day I'll start making money," Julian said gloomily—he knew he never would—"and you can have one of those jokes whenever you take the fit." But first they would move. He visualized a place where the nearest neighbors would be three miles away on either side.

"I think you're doing fine," she said, drawing on her gloves. "You've only been out of school a year. Rome wasn't built in a day."

She was one of the few members of the Y reducing class who arrived in hat and gloves and who had a son who had been to college. "It takes time," she said, "and the world is in such a mess. This hat looked better on me than any of the others, though when she brought it out I said, 'Take that thing back. I wouldn't have it on my head,' and she said, 'Now wait till you see it on,' and when she put it on me, I said, 'We-ull,' and she said, 'If you ask me, that hat does something for you and you do something for the hat, and besides,' she said, 'with that hat, you won't meet yourself coming and going.' "

Julian thought he could have stood his lot better if she had been selfish, if she had been an old hag who drank and screamed at him. He walked along, saturated in depression, as if in the midst of his martyrdom he had lost his faith. Catching sight of his long, hopeless, irritated face, she stopped suddenly with a grief-stricken look, and pulled back on his arm. "Wait on me," she said. "I'm going back to the house and take this thing off and tomorrow I'm going to return it. I was out of my head. I can pay the gas bill with that seven-fifty."

He caught her arm in a vicious grip. "You are not going to take it back," he said. "I like it."

Somerset Maugham was a master of having one character tell us what another character is like, as in this from his story "The Lotus Eater":

"He looked rather awful lying there in bed, with a week's growth of gray beard on his chin; but except for that funny look in his eyes he seemed quite normal."

"What funny look in his eyes?"

"I don't know exactly how to describe it. Puzzled. It's an absurd comparison, but suppose you threw a stone up in the air and it didn't come down but just stayed there. . . ."

"It would be rather bewildering," I smiled.

"Well, that's the sort of look he had."

No matter how humble their station or humdrum their life appears, we should strive above all when characterizing our protagonists to avoid the cliché, the stock character—the burly cop, the wise-cracking city editor, the whore with the heart of gold, the hard-hearted landlord, the siesta-taking Mexican, and the unconscionable used-car salesman.

Here again is John Leggett:

The stock character is easy to recognize, familiar to us from a lifetime of mediocre entertainment, yet difficult to avoid in storytelling. When a writer sets out to draw a character, it is second nature to reach up onto the shelf of our fictional experience for them.

What a fusty crowd is up there: the villain, the miser, the poor little rich girl, the country bumpkin, the indifferent clerk, the talkative cab-driver. As soon as we encounter one of their traits, say a downeast Maine twang, we can supply the rest of the formula: the man's economy with words, his diligence in mending his roof, his shrewdness and honesty, his suspicion of strangers.

It is their very predictability that makes these characters stale. We know that real people aren't that way. They are endlessly complex and never wholly predictable. What fascinates us and delights us most in fiction is the portrayal of characters who manage to confound our expectations and yet seem true to life.

When Scott Fitzgerald said that action is character he did not necessarily mean by action a sword fight, a murder, a walk across Niagara on a tightrope, or a car chase.

Study the quiet but important action in the following opening pages of John T. Lescroart's 1994 thriller *The 13th Juror*:

Jennifer Witt rechecked the table. It looked perfect, but when you never knew what perfect was, it was hard to be sure. There were two new red candles—Larry had a problem with half-burnt candles, with guttered wicks—in gleaming silver candlesticks.

She had considered having one red candle and one green candle since it was getting to be Christmas time. But Larry didn't like a jumble of colors. The living room was done all in champagne—which wasn't the easiest to keep clean, especially with a seven-year-old—but she wasn't going to change it. She remembered when she'd bought the Van Gogh print (A PRINT, FOR CHRIST'S SAKE! YOU'D HANG A PRINT IN MY LIVING ROOM?) and the colors had really bothered Larry.

He liked things ordered, exact. He was a doctor. Lives depended on his judgment. He couldn't get clouded up with junk in his own home, he told her.

So she went with the red candlesticks.

And the china. He liked the china, but then he'd get upset that things were so formal in their own home. Couldn't she just relax and serve them something plain on the white Pottery Barn stuff? Maybe just hot dogs and beans? They didn't have to eat gourmet every night. She tried hard to please, but with Larry, you never knew.

One time he wasn't in the mood for hot dogs and beans, he'd had an especially hard day, he said, and felt like some adult food. And Matt had had a bad day at school and was whining, and one of the plates had a chip in the side.

She shook her head to clear the memory.

Tonight she was making up with him, or trying to, so she decided to go with the china. She could feel his dissatisfaction . . . it got worse every time before he blew up . . . and she was trying to keep the explosion off for a few more days if she could.

So she'd fixed his favorite—the special veal kidney chops that you had to go get at Little City Meats in North Beach. And the December asparagus from Petrini's at $4.99 a pound. And she'd gotten Matt down early to bed.

She looked at herself in the mirror, thinking it odd that so many men thought she was attractive. Her nose had a hook halfway down the ridge. Her skin, to her, looked almost translucent, almost like a death mask. You could see all the bone structure, and she was too thin. And her eyes, too light a blue for her olive skin. Deep-set, somehow foreign-looking, as though her ancestors had come from Sicily or Naples instead of Milano, as they had.

She leaned over and looked more closely. There was still a broken vein, but the eyeshadow masked the last of the yellowish bruise. As she waited for him to come home, checking and rechecking, she had been curling her lower lip into her teeth again. Thank God she'd noticed the speck of coral lipstick on her tooth, the slight smear that had run beyond the edge of her liner.

There are so many things we can learn from this very professional writing.

Notice, though the main character is alone, she is not just sitting there musing and brooding on her life. That is a common and boring mistake that beginning writers make. Instead, she is *doing things* while she thinks. Something is happening and her actions, as well as her thoughts, tell us a great deal about her character and just as important about her husband. We see that Larry, besides just being a demanding and fussy husband, is also a dangerous one (the yellowish bruise), and this creates tension: what will happen to Jennifer when he gets home?

This is important:

**Half the battle of characterizing is making the
reader either like or dislike the character.**

In Lescroart's novel's opening we almost immediately like Jennifer. Why? *She is in trouble.*

Strange to say, while the average person in real life tries to avoid people in trouble, the books we enjoy are about people with problems, and the more severe the problem the greater appeal the story holds for us. How are they going to solve the problem? We immediately see that Jennifer is a nice person desperately trying to please an overbearing and abusive husband. In a like manner we dislike everything we know about Larry even before we meet him.

And also notice our old tried-and-true friend the mirror to tell us several things about Jennifer, her looks, her background, and her situation.

**Whenever possible try to link your similes with
some image compatible with the character
being described.**

Like Jessamyn West's simple but effective description of an Indian warrior in *The Massacre at Fall Creek*:

The grooves from his nose to his mouth were like runnels in clay land after a hard rain.

Or Sidney Sheldon's Frenchman in *The Other Side of Midnight*:

His hair was the color of the wet sand along the beaches of Normandy.

Sometimes writers don't need lengthy descriptions to characterize or individualize their fictional characters.

Take Browning's arrogant Duke of Ferrara in "My Last Duchess," who casually points out a portrait of his late young wife to a visitor and dismisses her callously with a sneering description:

"She had a heart too soon made glad."

John Cheever could individualize a character with a single line:

She was a pretty woman with that striking pallor you so often find in nymphomaniacs.

C. S. Lewis started his tale *The Voyage of the Dawn Treader* with:

There once was a boy by the name of Eustace Clarence Scrubb, and he almost deserved it.

In *The Disenchanted*, Budd Schulberg's hungover Scott Fitzgerald–like character is asked how he feels:

"Like a million dollars," Halliday said slowly, "in old Spanish doubloons buried ten feet underground."

Later the same character ruminates on his life and his Zelda-like wife:

> "The trouble with both of them was that they had thought youth was a career instead of a preparation."

Rafael Sabatini's opening line of *Scaramouche* individualized *and* characterized his hero:

> He was born with the gift of laughter and a sense that the world was mad.

Joseph Moncure March summed up a party girl:

> She could make a Baptist preacher choke with laughter over a dirty joke.

In a like manner, William Congreve wrote in 1695 in his play *Love for Love*:

> The jut of her bum would stir an anchorite.

And, of course, there's James Thurber's unforgettable description of the editor of *The New Yorker* magazine:

> He looked like a dishonest Abe Lincoln.

Brief and concise and slanted is this crisp description by Pat Conroy in his 1995 novel *Beach Music*:

> I tried to take the measure of the man sitting before me, but his tenseness made any casual study uncomfortable. Though controlled and disciplined even now, something rumbled just below the surface, bottled like a mean-spirited genie, ready for a turn toward malevolence. Even though

he was dressed in civilian clothes, a general's face shone hard as a diamond above his Brooks Brothers shirt. I knew that generalship was an art and a calling and an incurable illness. Arrogance is its natural resource and its favorite vacation is a fifteen-minute retreat to a full-length mirror.

"About today," the general said.

"Yes. Start with today."

No one has equaled Vladimir Nabokov for his deliciously succinct bit of back-story in *Lolita*:

My very photogenic mother died in a freak accident (picnic, lightning) when I was three.

The very opposite of brevity is the next selection. In his 1878 novel *The Return of the Native*, Thomas Hardy devoted some six pages to describing his heroine Eustacia Vye. It is a static description—that is, the character is not engaged in any specific action or scene in the plot.

As pure inventory of a single character this famous passage must be the longest in literature and is worth studying, though it would be a fatal mistake for a modern writer to emulate its length:

Eustacia Vye was the raw material of a divinity. On Olympus she would have done well with a little preparation. She had the passions and instincts which make a model goddess, that is, those which make not quite a model woman. Had it been possible for the earth and mankind to be entirely in her grasp for a while, had she handled the distaff, the spindle, and the shears at her own free will, few in the world would have noticed the change of government. There would have been the same inequality of lot, the same heaping up of favours here, of contumely there, the same generosity before justice, the same perpetual dilemmas, the same captious alternation of caresses and blows that we endure now.

She was in person full-limbed and somewhat heavy; without ruddiness, as without pallor; and soft to the touch as a cloud. To see her hair was to fancy that a whole winter did not contain darkness enough to form its shadow: it closed over her forehead like nightfall extinguishing the western glow.

Her nerves extended into those tresses, and her temper could always be softened by stroking them down. When her hair was brushed she would instantly sink into stillness and look like the Sphinx. If, in passing under one of the Egdon banks, any of its thick skeins were caught, as they sometimes were, by a prickly tuft of the large *Ulex Europæus*—which will act as a sort of hairbrush—she would go back a few steps, and pass against it a second time.

She had pagan eyes, full of nocturnal mysteries, and their light, as it came and went, and came again, was partially hampered by their oppressive lids and lashes; and of these the under lid was much fuller than it usually is with English women. This enabled her to indulge in reverie without seeming to do so: she might have been believed capable of sleeping without closing them up. Assuming that the souls of men and women were visible essences, you could fancy the colour of Eustacia's soul to be flame-like. The sparks from it that rose into her dark pupils gave the same impression.

The mouth seemed formed less to speak than to quiver, less to quiver than to kiss. Some might have added, less to kiss than to curl. Viewed sideways, the closing-line of her lips formed, with almost geometric precision, the curve so well known in the arts of design as the cima-recta, or ogee. The sight of such a flexible bend as that on grim Egdon was quite an apparition. It was felt at once that that mouth did not come over from Sleswig with a band of Saxon pirates whose lips met like the two halves of a muffin. One had fancied that such lip-curves were mostly lurking underground in the South as fragments of forgotten marbles. So fine were the lines of her lips that, though full, each corner of her mouth was as clearly cut as the point of a spear. This keenness of corner was only blunted when she was given over to sudden fits of gloom, one of the phases of the night-side of sentiment which she knew too well for her years.

Her presence brought memories of such things as Bourbon roses, rubies, and tropical midnights; her moods recalled lotus-eaters and the march in "Athalie"; her motions, the ebb and flow of the sea; her voice, the viola. In a dim light, and with a slight rearrangement of her hair, her general figure might have stood for that of either of the higher female deities. The new moon behind her head, an old helmet upon it, a diadem of accidental dewdrops round her brow, would have been adjuncts sufficient to strike the note of Artemis, Athena, or Hera respectively, with as close an approximation to the antique as that which passes muster on many respected canvases.

Whew!

So now you know about the fascinating Eustacia Vye—perhaps even more than you cared to know about the lady. And this goes on for five more pages!

Her name prompts us to add one more thing about individualizing:

The character's name individualizes him or her.
Choose your characters' names carefully.

Can you imagine Hardy's naming his character Jane Miller or Butterfly McQueen instead of Eustacia Vye?

The film actress Diana Dors's real name was Diana Fluck. Would you react the same to Hardy's heroine if she were named Eustacia Fluck?

Elmore Leonard has said that he cannot envision a character until he gives him or her a name. Once he had a very taciturn character in a story but upon changing his name the man "began talking and wouldn't shut up."

Proper names give readers an immediate clue to the character's persona and, sometimes, background:

Clem is not as sophisticated as Cyril.
Noël is no physical match for Butch.
Trixie would be more fun at a party than Maud.
Winston reads more than Morrie.
Tony drinks more than Anthony.
Duke will be braver in battle than Bruce.

On the other hand, naming characters "against type," as they say in Hollywood, can create interest, i.e., Bruce is a heavyweight contender, Trixie is a rocket scientist, and Duke is a lady mud wrestler.

Avoid similarity of names that might confuse the reader. Bob and Andy and Tom and Bill and Henry and Harry are all too similar to be in the same platoon; give some longer names, some nicknames, maybe even a foreign name. It would be easier to differentiate their characters and it would help individualize them if they were called, for example: Clayton, Turk, Canzoneri, Dog-Boy, Goldstone, and Frobisher.

Unless you are writing slapstick, avoid funny names. I knew a man in San Francisco whose real name was Zeppelin Wong, another named Charlemagne Tower. We also know that real people have names like Eurythmia Jones, Philander Beadle, Mercurochrome Hives, Dawn Trueheart, and Ima Hogg and Ura Hogg. But I would not choose any of these for names in a work of serious fiction.

And always be mindful of James Thurber's admonition:

Probably the most important thing I can tell you about writing is that if you call a character MacDonald on page one, under no circumstances should you on page twelve refer to him as MacIntosh.

CHAPTER FIVE

DIALOGUE

Even Alice asked rhetorically: "And what is the use of a book without pictures or conversation?"

Dialogue is perhaps the most potent weapon in the writer's arsenal, and because the weapon can blow up in a writer's face this chapter will be extensive.

Entire stories can—and have—been written in dialogue with little or no exposition.

Dialogue can perform so many functions:

1. It can establish the setting.
2. It can warn of impending disaster.
3. It can delineate character.
4. It can individualize the speaker.
5. It can cause laughter, terror, pathos, and empathy.
6. It can arouse suspense, suspension, curiosity, or the libido.
7. It can reveal hidden agendas and back-story.
8. It can tell a bald-faced lie, or reveal an eternal truth. It can entertain by itself.

In this chapter you will see examples of each of the above, and in some of the selections a combining of all those elements.

When Elmore Leonard spoke at the Santa Barbara Writers Conference he maintained that

All the information you need can be given in dialogue.

Elmore Leonard is himself a modern master of dialogue and most of his novels are told in exchanges of the most realistic nature.

Let us look at a fragment from his book *Freaky Deaky*. Chris Mankowski, a young bomb and explosives technician, is undergoing a routine psychiatric evaluation before being transferred to another section:

> The voice said, "You were in Vietnam?"
>
> "It doesn't seem to have a direct connection, though."
>
> "What doesn't?"
>
> "See, when I was over there I was assigned to a Recon-Intelligence platoon, working with mostly a bunch of ARVNs. You know what I mean? South Vietnamese, supposedly the good guys. One of my jobs was to interrogate prisoners they'd bring in and then recommend their disposition."
>
> "Meaning how to dispose of them?"
>
> "Meaning what to do with them. Let 'em go, send 'em back to Brigade . . . but that's not what I'm talking about. Well, it is and it isn't."
>
> There was a silence. Chris tried to think of the right words, ways to begin. *One sunny day I was sitting in the R and I hootch at Khiem Hanh. . . .*
>
> "The day I'm talking about, I was sent out to question a guy the ARVNs believed was working for the Viet Cong. An informer with a sack over his head had fingered the

guy and they pulled him out of his village. I got there, they have this old man standing barefoot on a grenade with the pin pulled, his toes curled around to hold the lever in place and his hands tied behind his back. I never saw anybody so scared in my life. They have him behind a mud wall that used to be part of a house, in case his foot slipped off and the grenade blew. I had to talk to the guy across the wall with my interpreter hunched down behind it; he refused to stand up. The rest of them, the ARVNs, they're off about thirty meters or so having a smoke. Anyway, I ask the old guy a few questions. He doesn't know anything about the VC, he's a farmer. He's crying, he's shaking he's so scared, trying to keep his foot on the grenade. He can't even name his own kids. I tell the ARVNs the guy's clean, come put the pin back in and let him go. By the time I cut him loose I look up, the fucking ARVNs are walking off, going home. I go after 'em part way, I'm yelling, 'Where's the goddamn *pin*?' They don't know. They point, 'It's over there somewhere, on the ground. I yell some more. 'Well, help me find the goddamned thing. We can't leave the guy like that.' One of them says, 'Tell him to pick it up and throw it away.' They didn't care. They walk off laughing, think it's funny. Some of those guys, they even knew the old man. They knew he wasn't VC, but they didn't care. They walked away." Chris paused. Man, just thinking about it . . .

"I crawled around looking for the pin, finally gave up. The old man's crying—there was no way he could handle that grenade. The only thing I could think of, have him step off, I'd pick it up quick and throw it. But I couldn't tell him what I wanted to do, my *fucking* interpreter was gone. I did try. I went through the motions; but you see he didn't understand. The poor guy couldn't think straight. The only thing I could do was walk up to him, push him aside and grab it. But I had to keep him calm. I walk up to him, I'm going, 'Don't worry, Papa. Nothing to get excited about.' I'm about as far from that door from him, he can't do it anymore. He comes running at me, lunges and grabs hold, and in the five seconds we had I couldn't get the guy off me. I could *not* get him off. I tried to *drag* him out of there. . . ." Chris stared at the doctor's diploma hanging on the bare institutional wall.

"The grenade blew with the old man hanging onto me. It killed him and tore up both of my legs. I was in-country fifteen weeks and out of the army."

There was a long silence followed by faint sounds, the serious young doctor tapping his ballpoint pen on the desk, clearing his throat.

"As you approached the old man, Sergeant Mankowski, were you aware of being afraid?"

"Was I *afraid*? Of course I was afraid, I was scared to death."

"All right, but you also felt, I believe, a deep hostility toward the ARVN soldiers."

I have got to get out of here, Chris thought.

Besides being entertaining to read, that excerpt gives us some of Chris's back story, which is essential to the novel. See how many of the other functions that we listed are represented in this exchange.

Dialogue can do so many things!

Suspense? Look at the suspense created by Thomas Harris in the following excerpt from his best seller *The Silence of the Lambs*.

The situation: Clarice Starling, a young trainee with the FBI, has wangled an interview with a dangerous serial killer and sociopath, the famed "Hannibal the Cannibal" Lecter. There is tension immediately between Clarice and Dr. Chilton, the head of the psychiatric ward of the prison:

They had passed through two more gates and left the natural light behind. Now they were beyond the wards where inmates can mix together, down in the region where there can be no window and no mixing. The hallway lights are covered with heavy grids, like the lights in the engine rooms of ships. Dr. Chilton passed beneath one. When their footfalls stopped, Starling could hear somewhere beyond the wall the ragged end of a voice ruined by shouting.

"Lecter is never outside his cell without wearing full restraints and a mouthpiece," Chilton said. "I'm going to show you why. He was a model of cooperation for the first year after he was committed. Security around him was slightly relaxed—this was under the previous administration, you understand. On the afternoon of July 8, 1976, he complained of a chest pain and he was taken to the dispensary. His restraints were removed to make it easier to give him an electrocardiogram. When the nurse bent over him, he did this to her." Chilton handed Clarice Starling a dog-eared photograph. "The doctors managed to save one of her eyes. Lecter was hooked up to the monitors the entire time. He broke her jaw to get at her tongue. His pulse never got over eighty-five, even when he swallowed it."

Starling didn't know which was worse, the photograph or Chilton's attention as he gleaned her face with fast grabby eyes. She thought of a thirsty chicken pecking tears off her face.

"I keep him in here," Chilton said, and pushed a button beside heavy double doors of security glass. A big orderly let them into the block beyond.

Starling made a tough decision and stopped just inside the doors. "Dr. Chilton, we really need these test results. If Dr. Lecter feels you're his enemy—if he's fixed on you, just as you've said—we might have more luck if I approached him by myself. What do you think?"

Chilton's cheek twitched. "That's perfectly fine with me.

You might have suggested that in my office. I could have sent an orderly with you and saved the time."

"I could have suggested it there if you'd briefed me there."

"I don't expect I'll see you again, Miss Starling—Barney, when she's finished with Lecter, ring for someone to bring her out."

Chilton left without looking at her again.

How could we not read on to meet this arch fiend along with Clarice? In and around the dialogue we get a few of Clarice's reactions which help us get to know her and to characterize her.

Playing around with the spelling of spoken words to individualize the speaker or what is being said or how it is being said can be rewarding.

This is from my novel *Matador*:

"Oh, that's a long way off," she said. Only it came out, "Hats ahong hay aw," because now she was looking into her compact mirror and applying lipstick.

Brian Alcorn in a 1994 article in the *Los Angeles Times* wrote amusingly of his conjugal nocturnal communications. Herewith some of his pillow talk:

Every night, we have this call-and-response, where the one of us who is already asleep interviews the one who is just coming to bed. The entire interview is conducted in sleep language.

"Jock door?" the sleeping one asks.

"Yes, the back door is locked."

"Dogzin?"

"Yes, dear, I brought the dog in."

"DP?"

"I don't know if he did or not. It's dark outside."

The next morning, the conversation goes something like this:

"Tie zit?"

"About 8."

"Ga gup."

"Yes, it's time for you to get up."

"DP?"

"In the dining room."

The longer you are together, the more sophisticated your sleep vocabulary becomes.

O. Henry also had fun with the dialogue in his 1909 short story "Supply and Demand" of which this is a small sample (a little of this style goes a long way):

"I meets a man one night," said Finch, beginning his story—"a man brown as snuff, with money in every pocket, eating schweinerknuckel in Schlagel's. That was two years ago, when I was a hose-cart driver for No. 98. His discourse runs to the subject of gold. He says that certain mountains in a country down South that he calls Gaudymala is full of it. He says the Indians wash it out of the streams in plural quantities.

" 'Oh, Geronimo!' says I. 'Indians! There's no Indians in the South,' I tell him, 'except Elks, Maccabees, and the buyers for the fall dry-goods trade. The Indians are all on the reservations,' says I.

" 'I'm telling you this with reservations,' says he. 'They ain't Buffalo Bill Indians; they're squattier and more pedigreed. They call 'em Inkers and Aspics, and they was old inhabitants when Mazuma was King of Mexico. They wash the gold out of the mountain streams,' says the brown man, 'and fill quills with it; and then they empty 'em into red jars till they are full; and then they pack it in buck-skin sacks of one arroba each—an arroba is twenty-five pounds—and store it in a stone house, with an engraving of a idol with marcelled hair, playing a flute, over the door.'

In O. Henry's day dialect stories were more popular than they are today. That is not to say that one should never try to approximate regional accents or slangy speech; but they are easily overdone and end up trying the reader's patience.

An example are the once-popular Uncle Remus stories, of which this is a small taste of a long-gone style:

> "Aha!" sez Brer Fox, sezee, "you'r dar, is you?" sezee. "Well I'm gwineter smoke you out, ef it takes a month. You'er mine dis time," sezee.
> Brer Rabbit ain't saying nothing.
> "Ain't you comin' down?" sez Brer Fox, sezee.
> Brer Rabbit ain't saying nothing.
> Then Brer Fox he went out after some wood, he did, and when he came back he heard Brer Rabbit laughing.
> "W'at you laughin' at, Brer Rabbit?" sez Brer Fox, sezee.
> "Can't tell you, Brer Fox," sez Brer Rabbit, sezee.
> "Bett tell, Brer Rabbit," sez Brer Fox, sezee.
> " 'Tain't nuthin' but a box er money somebody done gone an' lef' up here in de chink en de chimbly," sez Brer Rabbit, sezee.
> "Don't b'leeve you," sez Brer Fox, sezee.

A whole story in this dialect becomes tiring. But giving a touch of cockney ("It was a cane wif a 'orse's 'ead 'andle it was . . .") or Ozark ("If I'da known it was you I woulda retched out and wove . . .") or Transylvania ("Metapheezical purhops, bahloney purhops not . . .") is certainly accepted and adds flavor to dialogue, especially comedic conversation.

It is fun to write dialect and certainly *y'all, gonna, wanna, agin, y'know, hyar*, and dropping *g*'s and the like are valid to indicate the sound of colloquial or regional speech.

Dropping words altogether is part of realistic speech: "The hell you doin' this part of town, Mister?"

It's said that actions speak louder than words and perhaps they do. But what would a love scene be without words? What would Roxanne's lover, Christian, have done without Cyrano's words? And it wasn't Romeo's tights or sword play that captivated Juliet; it was all that fancy talk, balcony-wise.

David Mamet, one of today's foremost playwrights, maintains:

Tolstoy says that all happy families are alike, and every unhappy family is unhappy according to its own ways.*

I think the same is true of languages.

The language of love is, finally, fairly limited. "You're beautiful," "I need you," "I love you," "I want you." Love expresses itself, so it doesn't need a lot of words.

On the other hand, aggression has an unlimited vocabulary. The unhappy family has myriad ways in which to be unhappy, in which to torture its members. In a happy family, the denotations and connotations of words are fairly close to the surface. But in an unhappy family relationship/political situation/trial, you are dealing with an adversary, and you have to be on guard. You listen with a much more attenuated decimal point of meaning to gauge the other's intent.

---

*Author Susan Cheever says: "What Tolstoy is trying to tell us is that *all* families are unhappy."

Let's look at some examples of *love* dialogue first before we get to *aggression* and Mamet's "unlimited vocabulary."

F. Scott Fitzgerald's novel *Tender Is the Night* is believed by many people to be at least the equal of his more widely known *The Great Gatsby*. In the beginning of the novel the focus is on Rosemary Hoyt, a very young actress, Dick Diver, a doctor, and his wife Nicole.

Fitzgerald was proud of his descriptions of people and took care to make them economical but memorable. Before we hear these three people talk, let us see what they look like. These descriptions, which come several pages apart, are of (a) Rosemary, (b) Nicole, and (c) Dick.

A. The mother's face was of a fading prettiness that would soon be patted with broken veins; her expression was both tranquil and aware in a pleasant way. However, one's eye moved on quickly to her daughter, who had magic in her pink palms and her cheeks lit to a lovely flame, like the thrilling flush of children after their cold baths in the evening. Her fine forehead sloped gently up to where her hair, bordering it like an armorial shield, burst into lovelocks and waves and curlicues of ash blonde and gold. Her eyes were bright, big, clear, wet, and shining, the color of her cheeks was real, breaking close to the surface from the strong young pump of her heart. Her body hovered delicately on the last edge of childhood—she was almost eighteen, nearly complete, but the dew was still on her.

B. Nicole Diver, her brown back hanging from her pearls, was looking through a recipe book for chicken Maryland. She was about twenty-four, Rosemary guessed—her face could have been described in terms of conventional prettiness, but the effect was that it had been made first on the heroic scale with strong structure and marking, as if the features and vividness of brow and coloring, everything we associate with temperament and character had been molded with a Rodinesque intention, and then chiseled away in the direction of prettiness to a point where a single slip would have irreparably diminished its force and quality. With the mouth the sculptor had taken desperate chances—it was the cupid's bow of a magazine cover, yet it shared the distinction of the rest.

C. But Dick Diver—he was all complete there. Silently she admired him. His complexion was reddish and weather-burned, so was his short hair—a light growth of it rolled down his arms and hands. His eyes were of a bright, hard blue. His nose was somewhat pointed and there was never any doubt at whom he was looking or talking—and this is a flattering attention, for who looks at us?—glances fall upon us, curious or disinterested, nothing more. His voice, with some faint Irish melody running through it, wooed the world, yet she felt the layer of hardness in him, of self-control and of self-discipline, her own virtues. Oh, she chose him, and Nicole, lifting her head saw her choose him, heard the little sigh at the fact that he was already possessed.

Now let us hear Rosemary and Dick talk to each other the first time that they are really alone together:

"What is it you are giving up?" demanded Rosemary, facing Dick earnestly in the taxi.
"Nothing of importance."
"Are you a scientist?"
"I'm a doctor of medicine."
"Oh-h!" she smiled delightedly. "My father was a doctor too. Then why don't you—" she stopped.
"There's no mystery. I didn't disgrace myself at the

height of my career, and hide away on the Riviera. I'm just not practising. You can't tell, I'll probably practise again some day."

Rosemary put up her face quietly to be kissed. He looked at her for a moment as if he didn't understand. Then holding her in the hollow of his arm he rubbed his cheek against her cheek's softness, and then looked down at her for another long moment.

"Such a lovely child," he said gravely.

She smiled up at him; her hands playing conventionally with the lapels of his coat. "I'm in love with you and Nicole. Actually that's my secret—I can't even talk about you to anybody because I don't want any more people to know how wonderful you are. Honestly—I love you and Nicole—I do."

—So many times he had heard this—even the formula was the same.

Suddenly she came toward him, her youth vanishing as she passed inside the focus of his eyes and he had kissed her breathlessly as if she were any age at all. Then she lay back against his arm and sighed.

"I've decided to give you up," she said.

Dick started—had he said anything to imply that she possessed any part of him?

"But that's very mean," he managed to say lightly, "just when I was getting interested."

"I've loved you so—" As if it had been for years. She was weeping a little now. "I've loved you so-o-o."

Then he should have laughed, but he heard himself saying, "Not only are you beautiful but you are somehow on the grand scale. Everything you do, like pretending to be in love or pretending to be shy gets across."

In the dark cave of the taxi, fragrant with the perfume Rosemary had bought with Nicole, she came close again, clinging to him. He kissed her without enjoying it. He

knew that there was passion there, but there was no shadow
of it in her eyes or on her mouth; there was a faint spray
of champagne on her breath. She clung nearer desperately
and once more he kissed her and was chilled by the inno-
cence of her kiss, by the glance that at the moment of contact looked beyond him out into the darkness of the night,
the darkness of the world. She did not know yet that splendor is something in the heart; at the moment when she realized that and melted into the passion of the universe he
could take her without question or regret.

Her room in the hotel was diagonally across from theirs
and nearer the elevator. When they reached the door she
said suddenly:

"I know you don't love me—I don't expect it. But you
said I should have told you about my birthday. Well, I did,
and now for my birthday present I want you to come into
my room a minute while I tell you something. Just one
minute."

They went in and he closed the door, and Rosemary
stood close to him, not touching him. The night had drawn
the color from her face—she was pale as pale now, she was
a white carnation left after a dance.

"When you smile—" He had recovered his paternal attitude, perhaps because of Nicole's silent proximity, "I always think I'll see a gap where you've lost some baby
teeth."

But he was too late—she came close up against him
with a forlorn whisper.

"Take me."

"Take you where?"

Astonishment froze him rigid.

"Go on," she whispered. "Oh, please go on, whatever
they do. I don't care if I don't like it—I never expected
to—I've always hated to think about it but now I don't. I
want you to."

She was astonished at herself—she had never imagined she could talk like that. She was calling on things she had read, seen, dreamed through a decade of convent hours. Suddenly she knew too that it was one of her greatest rôles and she flung herself into it more passionately.

"This is not as it should be," Dick deliberated. "Isn't it just the champagne? Let's more or less forget it."

"Oh, no, *now*. I want you to do it now, take me, show me, I'm absolutely yours and I want to be."

"For one thing, have you thought how much it would hurt Nicole?"

"She won't know—this won't have anything to do with her."

He continued kindly.

"Then there's the fact that I love Nicole."

"But you can love more than just one person, can't you? Like I love Mother and I love you—more. I love you more now."

"—the fourth place you're not in love with me but you might be afterwards, and that would begin your life with a terrible mess."

"No, I promise I'll never see you again. I'll get Mother and go to America right away."

He dismissed this. He was remembering too vividly the youth and freshness of her lips. He took another tone.

"You're just in that mood."

"Oh, please, I don't care even if I had a baby. I could go into Mexico like a girl at the studio. Oh, this is so different from anything I ever thought—I used to hate it when they kissed me seriously." He saw she was still under the impression that it must happen. "Some of them had great big teeth, but you're all different and beautiful. I want you to do it."

"I believe you think people just kiss some way and you want me to kiss you."

"Oh, don't tease me—I'm not a baby. I know you're not in love with me." She was suddenly humble and quiet. "I didn't expect that much. I know I must seem just nothing to you."

"Nonsense. But you seem young to me." His thoughts added, "—there'd be so much to teach you."

Rosemary waited, breathing eagerly till Dick said: "And lastly things aren't arranged so that this could be as you want."

Her face drooped with dismay and disappointment and Dick said automatically, "We'll have to simply—" He stopped himself, followed her to the bed, sat down beside her while she wept. He was suddenly confused, not about the ethics of the matter, for the impossibility of it was sheerly indicated from all angles, but simply confused, and for a moment his usual grace, the tensile strength of his balance, was absent.

"I knew you wouldn't," she sobbed. "It was just a forlorn hope."

He stood up.

"Good night, child. This is a damn shame. Let's drop it out of the picture." He gave her two lines of hospital patter to go to sleep on. "So many people are going to love you and it might be nice to meet your first love all intact, emotionally too. That's an old-fashioned idea, isn't it?" She looked up at him as he took a step toward the door; she looked at him without the slightest idea as to what was in his head, she saw him take another step in slow motion, turn and look at her again, and she wanted for a moment to hold him and devour him, wanted his mouth, his ears, his coat collar, wanted to surround him and engulf him; she saw his hand fall on the doorknob. Then she gave up and sank back on the bed. When the door closed she got up and went to the mirror, where she began brushing her hair, sniffling a little. One hundred and fifty strokes Rosemary gave it, as usual, then a hundred and fifty more. She brushed it until her arm ached, then she changed arms and went on brushing. . . .

How much the author accomplishes here! By eavesdropping on their intimate conversation we learn so much about Rosemary's and Dick's characters.

And we even get a little laugh:

"Take me."
"Take you where?"

Recently I heard Neil Simon talk about his successful plays, and he emphasized that whether dealing with comedy or drama or a love scene, *every* scene must have overt or underlying *conflict*. The conflict in the foregoing Fitzgerald dialogue, though subtle, is clear, and at every turn it is bolstered by Dick Diver's thoughts. The events are seen from *his* point of view, through *his* eyes alone; Rosemary's thoughts are conveyed only by dialogue and her actions. ("Her face drooped with dismay and disappointment" . . . *NOT* merely "she was disappointed." *Show*, don't *tell.*)

Noël Coward's name is synonymous with witty dialogue, yet he rarely sacrifices the thrust of conflict or character development simply to make a bon mot or a quick quip. His 1930 play *Private Lives* is called a comedy, but there are many poignant love scenes, such as the following. The situation is that Amanda and Elyot, a divorced couple, are on their honeymoons on the Riviera with their new spouses. Not only are they staying at the same hotel, but they have adjoining suites.

(Remember that while it is unwise to *end* a story with a coincidence, one may *start* one with a coincidental happening.)

This is the dialogue that ensues when the protagonists find themselves alone for a few minutes on the moonlit porch:

There is dead silence for a moment.

AMANDA *(not looking at him)*: What have you been doing lately? During these last years?

ELYOT *(not looking at her)*: Travelling about. I went round the world you know after—

AMANDA *(hurriedly)*: Yes, yes, I know. How was it?

ELYOT: The world?

AMANDA: Yes.

ELYOT: Oh, highly enjoyable.

AMANDA: China must be very interesting.

ELYOT: Very big, China.

AMANDA: And Japan—

ELYOT: Very small.

AMANDA: Did you eat sharks' fins, and take your shoes off, and use chopsticks and everything?

ELYOT: Practically everything. *(He turns to her)*

AMANDA: And India, the burning Ghars, or Ghats, or whatever they are, and the Taj Mahal. How was the Taj Mahal?

ELYOT *(looking at her)*: Unbelievable, a sort of dream.

AMANDA *(facing him)*: That was the moonlight I expect, you must have seen it in the moonlight.

ELYOT *(never taking his eyes off her face)*: Yes, moonlight is cruelly deceptive.

AMANDA: And it didn't look like a biscuit box, did it? I've always felt that it might.

ELYOT *(quietly)*: Darling, darling, I love you so.

AMANDA: And I do hope you met a sacred Elephant. They're lint white, I believe, and very, very sweet.

ELYOT: I've never loved anyone else for an instant.

AMANDA *(raising her hand feebly in protest)*: No, no, you mustn't—Elyot—stop.

ELYOT: You love me, too, don't you? *(He moves to her)* There's no doubt about it anywhere, is there?

AMANDA: No, no doubt anywhere.

ELYOT: You're looking very lovely you know, in this damned moonlight, Amanda. Your skin is clear and cool, and your eyes are shining, and you're growing lovelier and lovelier every second as I look at you. You don't hold any mystery for me, darling, do you mind? There isn't a particle of you that I don't know, remember, and want.

AMANDA *(softly)*: I'm glad, my sweet.

ELYOT: More than any desire anywhere, deep down in my deepest heart I want you back again—please—

AMANDA: Don't say any more, you're making me cry so dreadfully.

Elyot pulls her gently into his arms and they stand silently, completely oblivious to everything but the moment, and each other. Then finally they separate.

What a lovely line is:

There isn't a particle of you that I don't know, remember, and want.

How could she resist? (She doesn't. They get back together.)

Quite different are the people and the situation in James M. Cain's 1934 blockbuster *The Postman Always Rings Twice*.

Frank Chambers is a twenty-four-year-old drifter who lands a job at a "roadside sandwich joint, like a million others in California," run by Nick Papadakis and his hormonal young wife, Cora:

Except for the shape, she really wasn't any raving beauty, but she had a sulky look to her, and her lips stuck out in a way that made me want to mash them in for her.

Within two short chapters they are lovers. In Chapter Three we learn something of Cora's character, background, and the fact that she is up to no good.

"Look out, Frank. You'll break a spring leaf."

"To hell with the spring leaf."

We were crashing into a little eucalyptus grove beside the road. The Greek had sent us down to the market to take back some T-bone steaks he said were lousy, and on the way back it had got dark. I slammed the car in there, and it bucked and bounced, but when I was in among the trees I stopped. Her arms were around me before I even cut the lights. We did plenty. After a while we just sat there. "I can't go on like this, Frank."

"Me neither."

"I can't stand it. And I've got to get drunk with you, Frank. You know what I mean? Drunk."

"I know."

"And I hate that Greek."

"Why did you marry him? You never did tell me that."

"I haven't told you anything."

"We haven't wasted any time on talk."

"I was working in a hash house. You spend two years in a Los Angeles hash house and you'll take the first guy that's got a gold watch."

"When did you leave Iowa?"

"Three years ago. I won a beauty contest. I won a high school beauty contest, in Des Moines. That's where I lived. The prize was a trip to Hollywood. I got off the Chief with fifteen guys taking my picture, and two weeks later I was in the hash house."

"Didn't you go back?"

"I wouldn't give them the satisfaction."

"Did you get in movies?"

"They gave me a test. It was all right in the face. But

they talk, now. The pictures, I mean. And when I began to talk, up there on the screen, they knew me for what I was, and so did I. A cheap Des Moines trollop, that had as much chance in pictures as a monkey has. Not as much. A monkey, anyway, can make you laugh. All I did was make you sick."

"And then?"

"Then two years of guys pinching your leg and leaving nickel tips and asking how about a little party tonight. I went on some of them parties, Frank."

"And then?"

"You know what I mean about them parties?"

"I know."

"Then he came along. I took him, and so help me, I meant to stick by him. But I can't stand it any more. God, do I look like a little white bird?"

"To me, you look more like a hell cat."

"You know, don't you. That's one thing about you. I don't have to fool you all the time. And you're clean. You're not greasy. Frank, do you have any idea what that means? You're not greasy."

"I can kind of imagine."

"I don't think so. No man can know what that means to a woman. To have to be around somebody that's greasy and makes you sick at the stomach when he touches you. I'm not really such a hell cat, Frank. I just can't stand it any more."

"What are you trying to do? Kid me?"

"Oh, all right. I'm a hell cat, then. But I don't think I would be so bad. With somebody that wasn't greasy."

"Cora, how about you and me going away?"

"I've thought about it. I've thought about it a lot."

"We'll ditch this Greek and blow. Just blow."

"Where to?"

"Anywhere. What do we care?"

"Anywhere. Anywhere. You know where that is?"

"All over. Anywhere we choose."

"No it's not. It's the hash house."

"I'm not talking about the hash house. I'm talking about the road. It's fun, Cora. And nobody knows it better than I do. I know every twist and turn it's got. And I know how to work it, too. Isn't that what we want? Just to be a pair of tramps, like we really are?"

"You were a fine tramp. You didn't even have socks."

"You liked me."

"I loved you. I would love you without even a shirt. I would love you specially without a shirt, so I could feel how nice and hard your shoulders are."

"Socking railroad detectives developed the muscles."

"And you're hard all over. Big and tall and hard. And your hair is light. You're not a little soft greasy guy with black kinky hair that he puts bay rum on every night."

"That must be a nice smell."

"But it won't do, Frank. That road, it don't lead anywhere but to the hash house. The hash house for me, and some job like it for you. A lousy parking lot job, where you wear a smock. I'd cry if I saw you in a smock, Frank."

"Well?"

She sat there a long time, twisting my hand in both of hers. "Frank, do you love me?"

"Yes."

"Do you love me so much that not anything matters?"

"Yes."

"There's one way."

"Did you say you weren't really a hell cat?"

"I said it, and I mean it. I'm not what you think I am, Frank. I want to work and be something, that's all. But you can't do it without love. Do you know that, Frank? Anyway, a woman can't. Well, I've made one mistake. And I've got to be a hell cat, just once, to fix it. But I'm not really a hell cat, Frank."

"They hang you for that."

"Not if you do it right. You're smart, Frank. I never fooled you for a minute. You'll think of a way. Plenty of them have. Don't worry. I'm not the first woman that had to turn hell cat to get out of a mess."

"He never did anything to me. He's all right."

"The hell he's all right. He stinks, I tell you. He's greasy and he stinks. And do you think I'm going to let you wear a smock, with Service Auto Parts printed on the back, Thank-U Call Again, while he has four suits and a dozen silk shirts? Isn't that business half mine? Don't I cook? Don't I cook good? Don't you do your part?"

"You talk like it was all right."

"Who's going to know if it's all right or not, but you and me?"

"You and me."

"That's it, Frank. That's all that matters, isn't it? Not you and me and the road, or anything else but you and me."

"You must be a hell cat, though. You couldn't make me feel like this if you weren't."

"That's what we're going to do. Kiss me, Frank. On the mouth."

I kissed her. Her eyes were shining up at me like two blue stars. It was like being in church.

No talk of the Taj Mahal in the moonlight here!

And a lesser writer might have devoted a chapter to what Cain does in the line: "We did plenty."

Did you notice that in this long excerpt there are no "he saids" or "she saids"? They are not necessary—the reader always knows who is talking.

And certainly there is no "he retorted" or "she sneered" or "she whispered" or "he said sarcastically" or "she chortled."

The *way* Frank and Cora say the dialogue is inherent in the words they speak.

If one had to characterize Cain's dialogue with a single phrase, it would be: *economical energy.*

John O'Hara wrote some of America's finest stories for a sophisticated magazine, *The New Yorker*, yet he did not always write about sophisticated people. But whatever the strata or social standing of his dramatis personae, he always captured the sound and flavor of their speech.

Frank MacShane, author of a biography of John O'Hara, has written so well of that writer:

O'Hara was not a satirist by nature; rather he had a fiction writer's interest in human character. For him, dialogue was a way of revealing human traits without spending much time on description and setting. He found that when he had a precinct cop pick up the telephone and say, "Wukkan I do fya?" he was able to depict the whole police station in those few words. When a teenage girl from Brearley or Chapin says, "Robert didn't come with she or I," she reveals in the grammatical error her breathless concern to appear grown-up.

"If people did not talk right, they were not real people," O'Hara observed when he was still a schoolboy, and it was as true of life as of art. "I do not believe," he later wrote, "that a writer who neglects or has not learned to write good dialog can be depended upon for accuracy in his understanding of character and his creation of characters."

Talk was, for O'Hara, the beginning of many of his stories. Often he would sit at his typewriter and start by thinking of a couple of faces he had seen. He would put the people together in a restaurant or on an airplane, and they would begin to talk. "I let them do small talk for a page or two," O'Hara explained, "and pretty soon they begin to come to life. They do so entirely through dialog. I start by knowing nothing about them except what I remember of their faces. But as they chatter away, one of them, and then the other, will say something that is so revealing that I recognize the signs of created characters. From then on it is a question of how deeply I want to interest myself in the characters."

Here is the last half of a 1963 O'Hara short story called "How Can I Tell You?" in which a car salesman, Mark McGranville, finds himself inexplicably depressed. He stops off at his neighborhood bar on his way home:

"Let me have a bourbon and soda, will you, Ernie?"

"Why sure. Is there anything the matter, Mark?"

"No. Why?"

"I don't know. You want any particular bourbon?"

"I wouldn't be able to tell the difference. You know that."

"Okay, okay," said Ernie. He pantomimed getting a kick in the behind and went to the bar to get Mark's drink. He returned with a small round tray on which were a highball glass, a shot glass with the bourbon, a small bottle of club soda. "There you are. That's Old Gutburner, the bar bourbon."

"Old what?"

"Gutburner. Old Gutburner. That's what Paul calls the bar bourbon. It ain't all that bad. You want some music?"

"Christ, no."

"You just want to sit here and nobody bother you. Okay," said Ernie. He walked away, spinning the inverted tray on his forefinger, and Mark had a couple of sips of his drink. He waited for some pleasant effect, and when none came, he finished the drink in a gulp. "Ernie? Bring me another shot, will you?"

"Right," said Ernie. He served a second shot glass of the bourbon. "You got enough soda there? Yeah, you got enough soda."

"I don't want any soda. I'm drinking this straight."

"Yeah, bourbon ought to be drunk straight. Bourbon has a flavor that if you ask me, you oughtn't to dilute it. That is, if you happen to like the taste of bourbon in the first place. Personally, I don't. I'll take a drink of bourbon, like if I'm at a football game to see the New York Giants. Or you take if I'm out in the woods, looking for deer, I usely take a pint of rye with me, or sometimes bourbon. It'll ward off the cold and the taste lasts longer. But for all-day drinking, I stick to scatch. You don't get tired of the taste of scatch. Your rye and your bourbon, they're too sweet if you're gonna drink all day. You know a funny thing about scatch, it's getting to be the most popular drink in France and Japan. That was in an article I read, this magazine I get. You know, in this business we get these magazines. I guess you have them in the car business. Trade publications, they're known as."

"Even the undertakers."

"Huh?"

"The undertakers have trade publications."

"They do, ah? Well, wuddia know. I guess every business has them."

"Every business is the same, when you come right down to it," said Mark McGranville.

"Well that's a new one on me. We're all in it for the money, but what's the same about selling cars and pushing Old Gutburner?"

"What you just said," said Mark McGranville. "We're all in it for the money. You. Me. Undertakers."

"You're talking like an I-don't-know-what," said Ernie.

"I know I am. What do I owe you?"

"Be—nothing," said Ernie.

"On the house?"

"Come in again when you'll get some enjoyment out of it. I don't want to take your money under these conditions."

"You, Ernie?"

"Yeah, me. You got sumpn eatin' you, boy, whatever it is."

"I know I have," said Mark McGranville. "Maybe it's the weather. I don't know."

"Well, my booze won't do it any good, Mark. I get days like this myself, once in a great while. The women get them all the time, but that's different. Take in a show tonight. You know this English fellow, with the big gap in his teeth. Terry?"

"Terry-Thomas."

"He's at the Carteret. He's always good for a laugh. You're not a booze man, Mark. Some are, but not you. You were taking it like medicine, for God's sake. Castor oil or something."

"Yeah. Well, thanks, Ernie. See you," said Mark McGranville.

He could not understand why he went through dinner and the entire evening without telling Jean about the T-Bird and the two Galaxies in one day. He knew that it was because he did not want to give her any good news; that much he understood. She would respond to the good news as she always did, enthusiastically and proudly, and he was in no mood to share her enthusiasm or accept the compliment of her pride in him. All that he understood, but he could not understand why he preferred to remain in this mood. She would cheer him up, and he did not want to be cheered up. He was perfunctory when the kids kissed him goodnight, and after the eleven o'clock news on the TV he rose, snapped the power dial, and went to the bedroom. He was in bed when Jean kissed him goodnight and turned out the light.

"Mark?" she said, from her bed.

"What?"

"Is there something the matter?"

"Nope."

"Goodnight," she said.

"Goodnight," said Mark McGranville.

Five, ten dark minutes passed.

"If you don't want to tell me," she said.

"How the hell can I tell you when I don't know myself?" he said.

"Oh," she said. "Shall I come over?"

"I just as soon you wouldn't," he said. "I don't know what it is."

"If I come over you'll sleep better," she said.

"Jean, please. It isn't that. Christ, I sold two Galaxies and a T-Bird today—"

"You *did*?"

"That ought to make me feel good, but I don't know what's the matter with me. I had a couple drinks at Ernie's, but nothing."

"I knew you had something to drink. It didn't show, but I could smell it."

"Oh, I'm not hiding anything."

"You hid it about the Galaxies and the T-Bird."

"I know I did. I'd have told you in the morning."

"All right. Goodnight."

"Goodnight," he said.

He thought his mind was busy, busy, busy, and that he had been unable to get to sleep, but at five minutes past two he looked at the radium hands of the alarm clock and realized that he must have slept for at least an hour, that some of the activity of his mind was actually dreams. They were not frightening dreams or lascivious ones; they were not much of anything but mental activity that had taken place while he thought he was awake but must have been asleep. Jean was asleep, breathing regularly. She made two musical notes in deep sleep, the first two notes of "Yes Sir That's My Baby"; the *yes* note as she exhaled, the *sir* as she drew breath. And yet he could tell, in spite of the dark, that she would be slightly frowning, dreaming or thinking, one or the other or both. He had so often watched her asleep, physically asleep, and making the musical notes of her regular breathing, but the slight frown revealing that her mind was at work, that her intelligence was functioning in ways that would always be kept secret from him, possibly even from herself. It was not that her sleeping face was a mask; far from it. The mask was her wakeful face, telling only her responses to things that happened and were said, the obvious responses to pleasant and unpleasant things in life. But in the frowning placidity of sleep her mind was naked. It did not matter that he could not read her thoughts; they were there, far more so than when she was awake.

He got out of bed and went to the warm living room and turned on one bulb in a table lamp. He lit a cigarette and took the first drag, but he let it go out. He was thirty years old, a good father, a good husband, and so well thought of that Mrs. Preston would make sure that he got credit for a sale. His sister had a good job, and his mother was taken care of. On the sales blackboard at the garage his name was always first or second, in two years had not been down to third. Nevertheless he went to the hall closet and got out his 20-gauge and broke it and inserted a shell.

He returned to his chair and re-lit the cigarette that had gone out, and this time he smoked rapidly. The shotgun rested with the butt on the floor, the barrel lying against his thigh, and he held the barrel loosely with the fingers of his left hand as he smoked. The cigarette was now down to an inch in length, and he crushed it carefully.

Her voice came softly. "Mark," she said.

He looked at the carpet. "What?" he said.

"Don't. Please?"
"I won't," he said.

This is not sparkling dialogue; it is not Noël Coward or Oscar Wilde.

This is commonplace dialogue, short sentences, simple dialogue, *believable* dialogue. Perhaps what is not said is more revealing than what is said.

And notice how the author himself does not just bluntly come out and say: "Mark McGranville was depressed."

How much more effective it is when the bartender says: "Is there anything the matter, Mark?" This involves the reader, makes us observers of a scene from life, eavesdroppers, not merely recipients of information fed us by a writer.

Mark answers: "No. Why?" But we know better because of Ernie's observation.

And the author reinforces our suspicions a little later with the bartender's:

"You got sumpn eatin' you, boy, whatever it is."

John O'Hara knew how to use the dialogue of a minor character to advance the plot and to characterize his protagonists.

A frequently asked question is "How much dialogue should there be?"

There is no formula for the ratio of the spoken word to exposition either in novels or short stories. Entire stories have been written in dialogue and others have been written without a word of dialogue. I know of no novels that have gone to either extreme, but they may exist.

Some stories call for a great deal of dialogue; a John Cheever cocktail party would indicate a lot of talk, in a Robinson Crusoe–type story one would expect less.

Let us look at a lovely little story by a master of dialogue which demonstrates exactly the right balance of talk and exposition.

This is Graham Greene's "A Shocking Accident," published in 1967 in a collection entitled *May We Borrow Your Husband?*:

1

Jerome was called into his housemaster's room in the break between the second and the third class on a Thursday morning. He had no fear of trouble, for he was a warden—the name that the proprietor and headmaster of a rather expensive preparatory school had chosen to give to approved, reliable boys in the lower forms (from a warden one became a guardian and finally before leaving, it was hoped for Marlborough or Rugby, a crusader). The housemaster, Mr. Wordsworth, sat behind his desk with an appearance of perplexity and apprehension. Jerome had the odd impression when he entered that he was a cause of fear.

"Sit down, Jerome," Mr. Wordsworth said. "All going well with the trigonometry?"

"Yes, sir."

"I've had a telephone call, Jerome. From your aunt. I'm afraid I have bad news for you."

"Yes, sir?"

"Your father has had an accident."

"Oh."

Mr. Wordsworth looked at him with some surprise. "A serious accident."

"Yes, sir?"

Jerome worshipped his father: the verb is exact. As man re-creates God, so Jerome re-created his father—from a restless widowed author into a mysterious adventurer who travelled in far places—Nice, Beirut, Majorca, even the

Canaries. The time had arrived about his eighth birthday when Jerome believed that his father either "ran guns" or was a member of the British Secret Service. Now it occurred to him that his father might have been wounded in "a hail of machine-gun bullets."

Mr. Wordsworth played with the ruler on his desk. He seemed at a loss how to continue. He said, "You knew your father was in Naples?"

"Yes, sir."

"Your aunt heard from the hospital today."

"Oh."

Mr. Wordsworth said with desperation, "It was a street accident."

"Yes, sir?" It seemed quite likely to Jerome that they would call it a street accident. The police, of course, had fired first; his father would not take human life except as a last resort.

"I'm afraid your father was very seriously hurt indeed."

"Oh."

"In fact, Jerome, he died yesterday. Quite without pain."

"Did they shoot him through the heart?"

"I beg your pardon. What did you say, Jerome?"

"Did they shoot him through the heart?"

"Nobody shot him, Jerome. A pig fell on him." An inexplicable convulsion took place in the nerves of Mr. Wordsworth's face; it really looked for a moment as though he were going to laugh. He closed his eyes, composed his features, and said rapidly, as though it were necessary to expel the story as rapidly as possible, "Your father was walking along a street in Naples when a pig fell on him. A shocking accident. Apparently in the poorer quarters of Naples they keep pigs on their balconies. This one was on the fifth floor. It had grown too fat. The balcony broke. The pig fell on your father."

Mr. Wordsworth left his desk rapidly and went to the

window, turning his back on Jerome. He shook a little with emotion.

Jerome said, "What happened to the pig?"

2

This was not callousness on the part of Jerome as it was interpreted by Mr. Wordsworth to his colleagues (he even discussed with them whether, perhaps, Jerome was not yet fitted to be a warden). Jerome was only attempting to visualize the strange scene and to get the details right. Nor was Jerome a boy who cried; he was a boy who brooded, and it never occurred to him at his preparatory school that the circumstances of his father's death were comic—they were still part of the mystery of life. It was later in his first term at his public school, when he told the story to his best friend, that he began to realize how it affected others. Naturally, after that disclosure he was known, rather unreasonably, as Pig.

Unfortunately his aunt had no sense of humour. There was an enlarged snap-shot of his father on the piano: a large sad man in an unsuitable dark suit posed in Capri with an umbrella (to guard him against sunstroke), the Faraglioni rocks forming the background. By the age of sixteen Jerome was well aware that the portrait looked more like the author of *Sunshine and Shade* and *Rambles in the Balearics* than an agent of the Secret Service. All the same, he loved the memory of his father: he still possessed an album filled with picture-postcards (the stamps had been soaked off long ago for his other collection), and it pained him when his aunt embarked with strangers on the story of his father's death.

"A shocking accident," she would begin, and the stranger would compose his or her features into the correct shape for interest and commiseration. Both reactions, of course, were false, but it was terrible for Jerome to see how suddenly, midway in her rambling discourse, the interest would become genuine. "I can't think how such things can be allowed in a civilized country," his aunt would say. "I suppose one has to regard Italy as civilized. One is prepared for all kinds of things abroad, of course, and my brother was a great traveller. He always carried a water-filter with him. It was far less expensive, you know, than buying all those bottles of mineral water. My brother always said that his filter paid for his dinner wine. You can see from that what a careful man he was, but who could possibly have expected when he was walking along the Via Dottore Manuele Panucci on his way to the Hydrographic Museum that a pig would fall on him?" That was the moment when the interest became genuine.

Jerome's father had not been a very distinguished writer, but the time always seems to come, after an author's death, when somebody thinks it worth his while to write a letter to *The Times Literary Supplement* announcing the preparation of a biography and asking to see any letters or documents or receive any anecdotes from friends of the dead man. Most of the biographies, of course, never appear— one wonders whether the whole thing may not be an obscure form of blackmail and whether many a potential writer of a biography or thesis finds the means in this way to finish his education at Kansas or Nottingham. Jerome, however, as a chartered accountant, lived far from the literary world. He did not realize how small the menace really was, nor that the danger period for someone of his father's obscurity had long passed. Sometimes he rehearsed the method of recounting his father's death so as to reduce the comic element to its smallest dimensions—it would be of no use to refuse information, for in that case the biographer would undoubtedly visit his aunt, who was living to a great old age with no sign of flagging.

It seemed to Jerome that there were two possible methods—the first led gently up to the accident, so well prepared that the death came really as an anticlimax. The chief danger of laughter in such a story was always surprise. When he rehearsed this method Jerome began boringly enough.

"You know Naples and those high tenement buildings? Somebody once told me that the Neapolitan always feels at home in New York just as the man from Turin feels at home in London because the river runs in much the same way in both cities. Where was I? Oh, yes, Naples, of course. You'd be surprised in the poorer quarters what things they keep on the balconies of those skyscraping tenements—not washing, you know, or bedding, but things like livestock, chickens or even pigs. Of course the pigs get no exercise whatever and fatten all the quicker." He could imagine how his hearer's eyes would have glazed by this time. "I've no idea, have you, how heavy a pig can be, but those old buildings are all badly in need of repair. A balcony on the fifth floor gave way under one of those pigs. It struck the third-floor balcony on its way down and sort of ricocheted into the street. My father was on the way to the Hydrographic Museum when the pig hit him. Coming from that height and that angle it broke his neck." This was really a masterly attempt to make an intrinsically interesting subject boring.

The other method Jerome rehearsed had the virtue of brevity.

"My father was killed by a pig."

"Really? In India?"

"No, in Italy."

"How interesting. I never realized there was pig-sticking in Italy. Was your father keen on polo?"

In course of time, neither too early nor too late, rather as though, in his capacity as a chartered accountant, Jerome had studied the statistics and taken the average, he became engaged to be married: to a pleasant fresh-faced girl of twenty-five whose father was a doctor in Pinner. Her name was Sally, her favourite author was still Hugh Walpole, and she had adored babies ever since she had been given a doll at the age of five which moved its eyes and made water. Their relationship was contented rather than exciting, as became the love affair of a chartered accountant; it would never have done if it had interfered with the figures.

One thought worried Jerome, however. Now that within a year he might himself become a father, his love for the dead man increased; he realized what affection had gone into the picture-postcards. He felt a longing to protect his memory, and uncertain whether this quiet love of his would survive if Sally were so insensitive as to laugh when she heard the story of his father's death. Inevitably she would hear it when Jerome brought her to dinner with his aunt. Several times he tried to tell her himself, as she was naturally anxious to know all she could that concerned him.

"You were very small when your father died?"

"Just nine."

"Poor little boy," she said.

"I was at school. They broke the news to me."

"Did you take it very hard?"

"I can't remember."

"You never told me how it happened."

"It was very sudden. A street accident."

"You'll never drive fast, will you, Jemmy?" (She had begun to call him "Jemmy.") It was too late then to try the second method—the one he thought of as the pig-sticking one.

They were going to marry quietly at a registry-office and have their honeymoon at Torquay. He avoided taking her to see his aunt until a week before the wedding, but then the night came, and he could not have told himself whether his apprehension was more for his father's memory or the security of his own love.

The moment came all too soon. "Is that Jemmy's father?" Sally asked, picking up the portrait of the man with the umbrella.

"Yes, dear. How did you guess?"

"He has Jemmy's eyes and brow, hasn't he?"

"Has Jerome lent you his books?"

"No."

"I will give you a set for your wedding. He wrote so tenderly about his travels. My own favourite is *Nooks and Crannies*. He would have had a great future. It made that shocking accident all the worse."

"Yes?"

How Jerome longed to leave the room and not see that loved face crinkle with irresistible amusement.

"I had so many letters from his readers after the pig fell on him." She had never been so abrupt before.

And then the miracle happened. Sally did not laugh. Sally sat with open eyes of horror while his aunt told her the story, and at the end, "How horrible," Sally said. "It makes you think, doesn't it? Happening like that. Out of a clear sky."

Jerome's heart sang with joy. It was as though she had appeased his fear forever. In the taxi going home he kissed her with more passion than he had ever shown, and she returned it. There were babies in her pale blue pupils, babies that rolled their eyes and made water.

"A week today," Jerome said, and she squeezed his hand. "Penny for your thoughts, my darling."

"I was wondering," Sally said, "what happened to the poor pig?"

"They almost certainly had it for dinner," Jerome said happily and kissed the dear child again.

An amazing little story, isn't it? What starts out as farcical and anecdotal becomes believable and even poignant.

And what a lovely line:

"There were babies in her pale blue pupils, babies that rolled their eyes and made water."

It's popular to say that films don't really need good dialogue, that it's strictly a visual medium, that the images carry the story. Here, on that subject, is a famous scene from Scott Fitzgerald's unfinished novel, *The Last Tycoon*.

Situation: Stahr, the young, powerful Hollywood producer, confronts one of his screenwriters, an English novelist:

Stahr smiled at Mr. George Boxley. It was a kindly fatherly smile Stahr had developed inversely when he was a young man pushed into high places. Originally it had been a smile of respect toward his elders, then as his own decisions grew rapidly to displace theirs, a smile so that they should not feel it—finally emerging as what it was: a smile of kindness sometimes a little hurried and tired, but always there, toward anyone who had not angered him within the hour. Or anyone he did not intend to insult aggressive and outright.

Mr. Boxley did not smile back. He came in with the air of being violently dragged though no one apparently had a hand on him. He stood in front of a chair and again it was as if two invisible attendants seized his arms and set him down forcibly into it. He sat there morosely. Even when he lit a cigarette on Stahr's invitation, one felt that the match was held to it by exterior forces he disdained to control.

Stahr looked at him courteously.

"Something not going well, Mr. Boxley?"

The novelist looked back at him in thunderous silence.

"I read your letter," said Stahr. The tone of the pleasant

young headmaster was gone. He spoke as to an equal, but with a faint two-edged deference.

"I can't get what I write on paper," broke out Boxley. "You've all been very decent but it's a sort of conspiracy. Those two hacks you've teamed me with listen to what I say but they spoil it—they seem to have a vocabulary of about a hundred words."

"Why don't you write it yourself?" asked Stahr.

"I have. I sent you some."

"But it was just talk, back and forth," said Stahr mildly. "Interesting talk but nothing more."

Now it was all the two ghostly attendants could do to hold Boxley in the deep chair. He struggled to get up; he uttered a single quiet bark which had some relation to laughter but none to amusement, and said:

"I don't think you people read things. The men are dueling when the conversation takes place. At the end one of them falls into a well and has to be hauled up in a bucket."

He barked again and subsided.

"Would you write that in a book of your own, Mr. Boxley?"

"What? Naturally not."

"You'd consider it too cheap."

"Movie standards are different," said Boxley hedging.

"Do you ever go to them?"

"No—almost never."

"Isn't it because people are always dueling and falling down wells?"

"Yes—and wearing strained facial expressions and talking incredible and unnatural dialogue."

"Skip the dialogue for a minute," said Stahr. "Granted your dialogue is more graceful than what these hacks can write—that's why we brought you out here. But let's imagine something that isn't either bad dialogue or jumping down a well. Has your office got a stove in it that lights with a match?"

"I think it has," said Boxley stiffly, "—but I never use it."

"Suppose you're in your office. You've been fighting duels or writing all day and you're too tired to fight or write any more. You're sitting there staring—dull, like we all get sometimes. A pretty stenographer that you've seen before comes into the room and you watch her—idly. She doesn't see you though you're very close to her. She takes off her gloves, opens her purse and dumps it out on a table—"

Stahr stood up, tossing his key-ring on his desk.

"She has two dimes and a nickle—and a cardboard match box. She leaves the nickle on the desk, puts the two dimes back into her purse and takes her black gloves to the stove, opens it and puts them inside. There is one match in the match box and she starts to light it kneeling by the stove. You notice that there's a stiff wind blowing in the window—but just then your telephone rings. The girl picks it up, says hello—listens—and says deliberately into the phone, 'I've never owned a pair of black gloves in my life.' She hangs up, kneels by the stove again, and just as she lights the match you glance around very suddenly and see that there's another man in the office, watching every move the girl makes—"

Stahr paused. He picked up his keys and put them in his pocket.

"Go on," said Boxley smiling. "What happens?"

"I don't know," said Stahr. "I was just making pictures."

Boxley felt he was being put in the wrong.

"It's just melodrama," he said.

"Not necessarily," said Stahr. "In any case, nobody has moved violently or talked cheap dialogue or had any facial expression at all. There was only one bad line, and a writer like you could improve it. But you were interested."

"What was the nickle for?" asked Boxley evasively.

"I don't know," said Stahr. Suddenly he laughed. "Oh, yes—the nickle was for the movies."

The two invisible attendants seemed to release Boxley. He relaxed, leaned back in his chair and laughed.

"What in hell do you pay me for?" he demanded. "I don't understand the damn stuff."

"You will," said Stahr grinning, "or you wouldn't have asked about the nickle."

We can enjoy the above scene not only for its content but for the excellence of the writing in between the excellent dialogue.

Of course, films *are* essentially visual, but the best films also have unforgettable dialogue—just let these lines flicker and dance through your memory:

"Rosebud."

"Frankly, my dear, I don't give a damn."

"Toto, this doesn't look like Kansas anymore."

"I don't have to show you no stinkin' badge!"

"Plastic!"

"Nobody's perfect."

"All right, Mr. DeMille, I'm ready for my close-up."

"Go ahead, make my day."

"The stuff that dreams are made of."

And so many others.

We can learn from the dialogue of the movies—the good movies, that is.

And speaking of good movies ... One of the most enduring films of all time is *Casablanca*. Certainly, as directed by Michael Curtiz, the 1942 film is visually flawless, though hardly as inspired in the imagery department as are *Citizen Kane* or *The Black Stallion* or *A River Runs Through It*.

No, it is the words, not the images, that stick in our hearts and minds and which make *Casablanca* timeless. Let's look at a few of the many gems written by the Epstein brothers and Howard Koch.

RENAULT: Round up the usual suspects.

RENAULT: And what in heaven's name brought you to Casablanca?
RICK: My health. I came to Casablanca for the waters.
RENAULT: Waters? What waters? We're in the desert.
RICK: I was misinformed.

YVONNE: Where were you last night?
RICK: That's so long ago, I don't remember.
YVONNE *(after a pause)*: Will I see you tonight?
RICK: I never make plans that far ahead.

RICK: How can you close me up? On what grounds?
RENAULT: I am shocked, *shocked* to find that gambling is going on in here!

RICK: Here's looking at you, kid.

Ilsa looks at him tenderly. Rick takes her in his arms, and kisses her hungrily. While they are locked in an embrace the dull boom of cannons is heard. Rick and Ilsa separate.

ILSA *(frightened, but trying not to show it)*: Was that cannon fire, or is it my heart pounding?

RICK: Just the same, you call the airport and let me hear you tell them. And remember, this gun's pointed right at your heart.

RENAULT *(as he dials)*: That is my least vulnerable spot.

RICK *(drunken nostalgia)*: I bet they're asleep in New York. I'll bet they're asleep all over America. *(pounds the table suddenly)* Of all the gin joints in all the towns in all the world, she walks into mine! *(irritably, to Sam)* What's that you're playing?

SAM *(who has been improvising)*: Just a little something of my own.

RICK: Well, stop it. You know what I want to hear.

SAM: No, I don't.

RICK: You played it for her and you can play it for me.

SAM: Well, I don't think I can remember it.

RICK: If she can stand it, I can. Play it!

SAM: Yes, boss.

Sam starts to play "As Time Goes By."

RICK: Louis, I think this is the beginning of a beautiful friendship.

Rick and Renault walk off together into the night.

Notice, in all these many examples of dialogue that we have seen in this chapter, that there is little flowery language and certainly no big fancy words to look up in a dictionary.

Here are some dialogue tips:

> After writing down what must be conveyed in your dialogue, try reading it aloud, perhaps to another person.
> Does it sound stilted or does it seem natural? (Remember, most of us modern mortals tend to talk in short choppy sentences—and not always in perfect ones with nouns and verbs and adjectives in proper order.)
> Is the dialogue consistent with the character who speaks it?
> Does the dialogue advance the plot?
> Does it characterize the speaker or another character?
> Does it help us *see* what is going on?
> Does it create suspense or curiosity?
> Can some of the less important talk be put into "summary dialogue" so as not to tax the reader's attention unduly with mundane trivia? (Example: "After asking pleasantly for some minutes about Bill's family and his job, Clara said quietly: 'Why did you kill him, Bill?' ")
> Jot down overheard snatches of conversation in a restaurant, theater, or bus. Xerox good bits of dialogue garnered from the newspapers, TV, or the films.
> Copy choice selections of dialogue from favorite books and put them in your notebook.

Above all:

Train yourself to listen!

CHAPTER SIX

~

ROMANTIC ENCOUNTERS

How should your lovers meet?

There is no set formula nor should there be; the first meeting should come naturally out of the protagonist's characters and the situation and the circumstances.

The playwright George Axelrod and the legendary director Billy Wilder used to start each day with mental warming-up exercises to prepare for the serious work ahead. One favorite was "meet-cutes"—gimmicks whereby the leading man and the leading lady meet each other in an unusual manner. Gary Cooper and Claudette Colbert are both in a department store shopping for pajamas. He wants only the bottoms; she wants only the tops. They meet and fall in love. Another "meet-cute" involves a psychiatrist and a prostitute who both send their couches out to be recovered. The store mixes up the return deliveries. The two meet. They fall in love.

In still another, Audrey Hepburn is in her bed, late at night, working a crossword puzzle. She is the wife of England's ambassador to the United States. She picks up the telephone, calls the Russian embassy, and asks for someone who can give her assistance. It is Yul Brynner who answers the phone.

Hepburn politely asks Stalin's middle name. Brynner angrily replies, "We are not here for such nonsense." He hears Hepburn's distinctive tinkling laugh and bangs down the phone. The next night at a large ball Brynner hears that laugh. Looking up, he sees Hepburn, walks over to her, and says, "Ilyich." They fall in love.

In Hemingway's *For Whom the Bell Tolls*, Robert Jordan and Maria do not meet cute—they meet logically out of the circumstances. As an idealistic young American, Jordan has come to Spain to fight in that country's civil war. Maria is a victim of that war but a survivor of jail and rape. Their meeting takes place outside of a cave in the mountains near Madrid:

> Robert Jordan drank half the cup of wine but the thickness still came in his throat when he spoke to the girl.
>
> "How art thou called?" he asked. Pablo looked at him quickly when he heard the tone of his voice. Then he got up and walked away.
>
> "Maria. And thee?"
>
> "Roberto. Have you been long in the mountains?"
>
> "Three months."
>
> "Three months?" He looked at her hair, that was as thick and short and rippling when she passed her hand over it, now in embarrassment, as a grain field in the wind on a hillside. "It was shaved," she said. "They shaved it regularly in the prison at Valladolid. It has taken three months to grow to this. I was on the train. They were taking me to the south. Many of the prisoners were caught after the train was blown up but I was not. I came with these."

They became lovers soon after this meeting.

Madame Bovary, in Flaubert's eponymous novel, meets her first lover, Rodolphe, in her doctor husband's clinic. There are many tricks to be learned from Flaubert's skillful presentation of this scene. For example, the author himself does not *tell* us that Emma is beautiful, that Emma is unhappily married to an "oaf," and that she longs for love; Flaubert *shows*—rather than *tells*—us these things through the thoughts and observations of Rodolphe Boulanger. He also nails down the character, position, and intentions of Monsieur Boulanger, and we know that little good can come of this meeting.

Notice, also, that while up to now in the novel we have seen her life through Emma's and Charles's eyes, we switch easily into Rodolphe's point of view:

Emma was leaning out of her window—where she was often to be found, for in the country the window takes the place of theatres and park parades—and was amusing herself surveying the herd of yokels down below, when she saw a gentleman in a green velvet frock-coat. He wore yellow gloves, though his legs were clad in sturdy gaiters; and he was steering his way towards the doctor's house, followed by a peasant walking pensively with his eyes on the ground.

"Can I see the doctor?" he inquired of Justin, who was talking to Félicité on the doorstep. Taking him for the doctor's servant he added, "Tell him it's Monsieur Rodolphe Boulanger, of La Huchette."

It was no pride in his demesne that prompted the newcomer to add "of La Huchette," but simply the desire to make himself known. La Huchette was in point of fact a large estate near Yonville, of which he had just acquired the house, along with a couple of farms that he was working himself in a semi-serious manner.

He was a bachelor and said to be worth "at least six hundred a year."

Charles came into the dining-room. Monsieur Boulanger

presented his man, who wanted to be bled because he'd got "pins and needles all over."

"It'll clear me," was his answer to all arguments.

So Bovary sent for a bandage and a basin, which he asked Justin to hold.

"Don't be afraid, my man," he said to the already white-faced villager.

"No, no, go ahead!" the man answered. And he held out his brawny arm with a touch of bravado. At the prick of the lancet the blood spurted out and splashed against the mirror.

"Nearer with the basin!" Charles exclaimed.

"Lookee!" said the peasant. "It's like a young fountain flowing! What red blood I've got. Should be a good sign, eh?"

"Sometimes," the Officer of Health remarked, "they don't feel anything at first: the syncope occurs afterwards, especially with strong chaps like this."

Instantly the yokel let go of the lancet-case which he had been twirling in his fingers: a jerk of his shoulders snapped the back of his chair: his cap fell to the floor.

"I thought as much," said Bovary, putting his fingers over the vein.

The basin began to wobble in Justin's hands. He quaked at the knees. His face went white.

"Emma!" Charles called out, "Emma!"

She was down the stairs in a flash.

"Vinegar!" he cried. "Good Lord, two at once!"

He was so agitated, he had difficulty in applying the compress.

"It's nothing," said Monsieur Boulanger quite calmly, as he lifted Justin in his arms and set him down on the table with his back to the wall.

Madame Bovary began to untie his cravat. There was a

knot in his shirt-strings, and she was some minutes plying her dainty fingers at the lad's neck. Then she poured vinegar on to his cambric handkerchief, dabbed it over his forehead and blew on it delicately.

The man had come to. Justin remained unconscious, his pupils vanishing into the white of his eyes like blue flowers in milk.

"Don't let him see that," said Charles.

Madame Bovary picked up the basin. As she bent down to put it under the table, her dress, a yellow summer dress with four flounces, long in the waist and full in the skirt, spread out around her on the floor. Emma put out her arms to steady herself as she crouched down, and the material clung to her here and there following the curve of her bosom. . . .

Having re-tied his cravat, Justin made off, and they started talking about fainting fits. Madame Bovary had never had one.

"That's remarkable for a lady!" said Monsieur Boulanger. "You do find some very delicate people about, though. Do you know I've seen one of the seconds at a duel lose consciousness merely through hearing the pistols being loaded!"

"I'm not affected at all," said the chemist, "by the sight of other people's blood, but the mere idea of seeing my own flowing would be enough to make me faint, if I thought about it too much."

Monsieur Boulanger now sent his man off, telling him not to worry, since his whim had been gratified.

"It's given me the pleasure of your acquaintance," he added; and his eyes were on Emma as he spoke.

Then he deposited three francs on the edge of the table, bowed carelessly, and went.

He was soon over the river, on his way back to La

Huchette, and Emma watched him striding across the meadow, under the poplars, every now and then slowing up like one in thought.

"Very nice!" he was saying to himself. "Very nice, this doctor's wife! Pretty teeth, dark eyes, trim little foot, turned out like a Parisian! Where the deuce can she have come from? Where can that clumsy oaf have found her?"

Monsieur Rodolphe was thirty-four years old, hard of heart and shrewd of head, with much experience and understanding of women. This one had attracted him; so his mind was occupied with her, and with her husband.

"A stupid creature, he looks. Of course she's sick of him. Dirty nails and three days' growth of beard! . . . While he trots off on his rounds, she sits and darns the socks. And is bored! Longs to live in town and dance the polka every night! Poor little thing! Gasping for love, as a carp on a kitchen table for water. Three pretty words, and she'd adore you, I'll be bound. Tender, charming it'd be . . . Yes, but how to shake it off afterwards?"

The drawbacks to pleasure, glimpsed in advance, set him thinking by contrast of his mistress. This was an actress at Rouen, whom he kept. Seeing her in his mind's eye—sated at the very thought of her—he said to himself:

"Madame Bovary is far prettier—fresher, above all! Virginie has been getting decidedly too fat. She's so tiresome, with her wants. And her mania for prawns . . ."

Notice also that something else is going on in the scene besides just the two future lovers' meeting:

Each character has his own agenda.

Now here is another meeting—far more innocent. Tom Sawyer encounters Becky Thatcher and instantly experiences true love.

And how do we know he's in love, why do we believe it is love? Not because of anything the author *tells* us but what he *shows* us; anyone who willingly suffers corporal punishment just to sit next to a girl is incontrovertibly smitten!

Twain, an incomparable storyteller, knew that the more the author stays out of the picture and lets his characters act out their parts to *show* the reader what is going on—the better:

When Tom reached the little isolated frame schoolhouse, he strode in briskly, with the manner of one who had come with all honest speed. He hung his hat on a peg and flung himself into his seat with businesslike alacrity. The master, throned on high in his great splint-bottom arm-chair, was dozing, lulled by the drowsy hum of study. The interruption roused him.

"Thomas Sawyer!"

Tom knew that when his name was pronounced in full, it meant trouble.

"Sir!"

"Come up here. Now, sir, why are you late again, as usual?"

Tom was about to take refuge in a lie, when he saw two long tails of yellow hair hanging down a back that he recognized by the electric sympathy of love; and by that form was *the only vacant place* on the girls' side of the schoolhouse. He instantly said:

"I STOPPED TO TALK WITH HUCKLEBERRY FINN!" The master's pulse stood still, and he stared helplessly. The buzz of study ceased. The pupils wondered if this foolhardy boy had lost his mind. The master said:

"You—you did what?"

"Stopped to talk with Huckleberry Finn."

There was no mistaking the words.

"Thomas Sawyer, this is the most astounding confession I have ever listened to. No mere ferule will answer for this offense. Take off your jacket."

The master's arm performed until it was tired and the stock of switches notably diminished. Then the order followed:

"Now, sir, go and sit with the *girls*! And let this be a warning to you."

The titter that rippled around the room appeared to abash the boy, but in reality that result was caused rather more by his worshipful awe of his unknown idol and the dread pleasure that lay in his high good fortune. He sat down upon the end of the pine bench and the girl hitched herself away from him with a toss of her head. Nudges and winks and whispers traversed the room, but Tom sat still, with his arms upon the long, low desk before him, and seemed to study his book.

By and by attention ceased from him, and the accustomed school murmur rose upon the dull air once more. Presently the boy began to steal furtive glances at the girl. She observed it, "made a mouth" at him and gave him the back of her head for the space of a minute. When she cautiously faced around again, a peach lay before her. She thrust it away. Tom gently put it back. She thrust it away again, but with less animosity. Tom patiently returned it to its place. Then she let it remain. Tom scrawled on his slate, "Please take it—I got more." The girl glanced at the words, but made no sign. Now the boy began to draw something on the slate, hiding his work with his left hand. For a time the girl refused to notice; but her human curiosity presently began to manifest itself by hardly perceptible signs. The boy worked on, apparently unconscious. The girl made a sort of non-committal attempt to see it, but the boy did not betray that he was aware of it. At last she gave in and hesitatingly whispered:

"Let me see it."

Tom partly uncovered a dismal caricature of a house with two gable ends to it and a corkscrew of smoke issuing from the chimney. Then the girl's interest began to fasten itself upon the work and she forgot everything else. When it was finished, she gazed a moment, then whispered:

"It's nice—make a man."

The artist erected a man in the front yard, that resembled a derrick. He could have stepped over the house; but the girl was not hypercritical; she was satisfied with the monster, and whispered:

"It's a beautiful man—now make me coming along."

Tom drew an hour-glass with a full moon and straw limbs to it and armed the spreading fingers with a portentous fan. The girl said:

"It's ever so nice—I wish I could draw."

"It's easy," whispered Tom, "I'll learn you."

"Oh, will you? When?"

"At noon. Do you go home to dinner?"

"I'll stay if you will."

"Good—that's a whack. What's your name?"

"Becky Thatcher. What's yours? Oh, I know. It's Thomas Sawyer."

"That's the name they lick me by. I'm Tom when I'm good. You call me Tom, will you?"

"Yes."

Compare Tom's meeting Becky—simple and direct, no frills—with Charles Dickens's flamboyant account of David Copperfield's first meeting with the girl who will become his wife. In its Victorian style it would appear to be more *tell* than *show*, yet by informing us of the immediate daze the young lover fell into—so that he didn't know or care whose voice introduced him to the girl or remember what he ate at dinner, and so forth—the author *shows* us that our hero is in-deed in love.

There was a lovely garden to Mr. Spenlow's house; and though that was not the best time of the year for seeing a garden, it was so beautifully kept, that I was quite enchanted. There was a charming lawn, there were clusters of trees, and there were perspective walks that I could just distinguish in the dark, arched over with trellis-work, on which shrubs and flowers grew in the growing season. "Here Miss Spenlow walks by herself," I thought. "Dear me!"

We went into the house, which was cheerfully lighted up, and into a hall where there were all sorts of hats, caps, great-coats, plaids, gloves, whips, and walking-sticks. "Where is Miss Dora?" said Mr. Spenlow to the servant. "Dora!" I thought. "What a beautiful name!"

We turned into a room near at hand (I think it was the identical breakfast-room made memorable by the brown East India sherry), and I heard a voice say, "Mr. Copper-field, my daughter Dora, and my daughter Dora's confiden-tial friend!" It was, no doubt, Mr. Spenlow's voice; but I didn't know it, and I didn't care whose it was. All was over in a moment. I had fulfilled my destiny. I was a captive and a slave. I loved Dora Spenlow to distraction!

She was more than human to me. She was a Fairy, a Sylph, I don't know what she was—anything that no one ever saw, and everything that everybody ever wanted. I was swallowed up in an abyss of love in an instant. There was no pausing on the brink—no looking down, or looking back; I was gone, headlong, before I had sense to say a word to her. . . .

I don't remember who was there, except Dora. I have not the least idea what we had for dinner, besides Dora. My impression is, that I dined off Dora entirely, and sent away half a dozen plates untouched. I sat next to her. I talked to her. She had the most delightful little voice, the gayest little laugh, the pleasantest and most fascinating little ways, that ever led a lost youth into hopeless slavery.

What follows is an encounter radically different from the previous ones, a meeting of a man and woman which forever altered the way writers would write about sex. Its hard, naturalistic style and attitude is a breakaway from the idealistic and sugarcoated encounters of the Victorian era.

The novel is D. H. Lawrence's *Lady Chatterley's Lover*, which appeared in 1928. While it shocked the reading world back then with its candor, there is little of the sensational in it that one cannot find in many of today's best-sellers. The quality of Lawrence's writing, however, is still far above most of the current derivative novels.

Notice Lawrence's meticulous attention to detail in the scene. Also notice that what interests us here is not so much the action—a man washing himself—but Lady Chatterley's reaction to this commonplace function.

In a story, reaction is nearly always as important as action!

Notice also that while we see nearly everything from *her* point of view, the author had no qualms about slipping into the gamekeeper's mind for one brief sentence:

As she came out of the wood on the north side, the keeper's cottage, a rather dark, brown stone cottage, with gables and a handsome chimney, looked uninhabited, it was so silent and alone. But a thread of smoke rose from the chimney, and the little railed-in garden in the front of the house was dug and kept very tidy. The door was shut.

Now she was here she felt a little shy of the man, with his curious far-seeing eyes. She did not like bringing him orders, and felt like going away again. She knocked softly, no one came. She knocked again, but still not loudly. There was no answer. She peeped through the window, and saw the dark little room, with its almost sinister privacy, not wanting to be invaded.

She stood and listened, and it seemed to her she heard sounds from the back of the cottage. Having failed to make herself heard, her mettle was roused, she would not be defeated.

So she went round the side of the house. At the back of the cottage the land rose steeply, so the backyard was sunken, and enclosed by a low stone wall. She turned the corner of the house and stopped. In the little yard two paces beyond her, the man was washing himself, utterly unaware. He was naked to the hips, his velveteen breeches slipping down over his slender loins. And his white slim back was curved over a big bowl of soapy water, in which he ducked his head, shaking his head with a queer, quick little motion, lifting his slender white arms, and pressing the soapy water from his ears, quick, subtle as a weasel playing with water, and utterly alone. Connie backed away round the corner of the house, and hurried away to the wood. In spite of herself, she had had a shock. After all, merely a man washing himself; commonplace enough, Heaven knows!

Yet in some curious way it was a visionary experience: it had hit her in the middle of the body. She saw the clumsy breeches slipping down over the pure, delicate, white loins, the bones showing a little, and the sense of aloneness, of a creature purely alone, overwhelmed her. Perfect, white, solitary nudity of a creature that lives alone, and inwardly alone. And beyond that, a certain beauty of a pure creature. Not the stuff of beauty, not even the body of beauty, but a lambency, the warm, white flame of a single life, revealing itself in contours that one might touch: a body!

Connie had received the shock of vision in her womb, and she knew it; it lay inside her. But with her mind she was inclined to ridicule. A man washing himself in a back-yard! No doubt with evil-smelling yellow soap!—She was rather annoyed; why should she be made to stumble on these vulgar privacies?

So she walked away from herself, but after a while she sat down on a stump. She was too confused to think. But in the coil of her confusion, she was determined to deliver her message to the fellow. She would not be balked. She must give him time to dress himself, but not time to go out. He was probably preparing to go out somewhere.

So she sauntered slowly back, listening. As she came near, the cottage looked just the same. A dog barked, and she knocked at the door, her heart beating in spite of her-self.

She heard the man coming lightly downstairs. He opened the door quickly, and startled her. He looked un-easy himself, but instantly a laugh came on his face.

"Lady Chatterley!" he said. "Will you come in?"

His manner was so perfectly easy and good, she stepped over the threshold into the rather dreary little room.

"I only called with a message from Sir Clifford," she said in her soft, rather breathless voice.

The man was looking at her with those blue, all-seeing eyes of his, which made her turn her face aside a little. He thought her comely, almost beautiful, in her shyness, and he took command of the situation himself at once.

"Would you care to sit down?" he asked, presuming she would not. The door stood open.

"No thanks! Sir Clifford wondered if you would . . ." and she delivered her message, looking unconsciously into his eyes again. And now his eyes looked warm and kind, particularly to a woman, wonderfully warm, and kind, and at ease.

"Very good, your Ladyship. I will see to it at once."

Taking an order, his whole self had changed, glazed over with a sort of hardness and distance. Connie hesitated, she ought to go. But she looked round the clean, tidy, rather dreary little sitting-room with something like dismay.

"Do you live here quite alone?" she asked.

"Quite alone, your Ladyship."

And so the scene is set for one of literature's steamiest love affairs.

An author who was one of Sinclair Lewis's and Ernest Hemingway's favorites was James M. Cain. Perhaps best known for *The Postman Always Rings Twice*, he has influenced a generation of hard-boiled writers, such as Ross Macdonald, Robert B. Parker, and Elmore Leonard.

What follows is the opening of Cain's sensational 1937 novel *Serenade* in which the protagonist meets the unlikely but intriguing heroine. The Tupinamba, long gone, was an actual bar at 44 Bolivar Street in Mexico City, and I can attest that Cain has painted an accurate portrait of the place.

I was in the Tupinamba, having a *bizcocho* and coffee, when this girl came in. Everything about her said Indian, from the maroon *rebozo* to the black dress with purple flowers on it, to the swaying way she walked, that no woman ever got without carrying pots, bundles, and baskets on her head from the time she could crawl. But she wasn't any of the colors that Indians come in. She was almost white, with just the least dip of *café con leche*. Her shape was Indian, but not ugly. Most Indian women have a rope of muscle over their hips that give them a high-waisted, mis-shaped look, thin, bunchy legs, and too much breast-works. She had plenty in that line, but her hips were round, and her legs had a soft line to them. She was slim, but there was something voluptuous about her, like in three or four years she would get fat. All that, though, I only half saw. What I noticed was her face. It was flat, like an Indian's but the nose broke high, so it kind of went with the way she held her head, and the eyes weren't dumb, with that shiny, shoe-button look. They were pretty big, and black, but they leveled out straight, and had kind of a sleepy, impudent look to them. Her lips were thick, but pretty, and of course had plenty of lipstick on them.

It was about nine o'clock at night, and the place was pretty full, with bullfight managers, agents, newspaper men, pimps, cops and almost everybody you can think of, except somebody you would trust with your watch. She went to the bar and ordered a drink, then went to a table and sat down, and I had a stifled feeling I had had before, from the thin air up there, but that wasn't it this time. There hadn't been any woman in my life for quite some while, and I knew what this meant. Her drink came, and it was coca-cola and Scotch, and I thought that over. It might mean that she was just starting the evening, and it might mean she was just working up an appetite, and if it meant that I was sunk. The Tupinamba is more of a café than a restaurant, but plenty of people eat there, and if that was what she expected to do, my last three pesos wouldn't go very far.

I had about decided to take a chance and go over there when she moved. She slipped over to a place about two tables away, and then she moved again, and I saw what she was up to. She was closing in on a bullfighter named Triesca, a kid I had seen a couple of times in the ring, once when he was on the card with Solorzano, that seemed to be their main ace at the time, and once after the main season was over, when he killed two bulls in a novillada they had one Sunday in the rain. He was a wow with the cape, and just moving up into the money. He had on the striped suit a Mexican thinks is pretty nifty, and a cream-colored hat. He was alone, but the managers, agents, and writers kept dropping by his table. She didn't have much of a chance, but every time three or four or five of them would shove off she would slip nearer. Pretty soon she dropped down beside him. He didn't take off his hat. That ought to have told me something, but it didn't. All I saw was a cluck too stuck on himself to know how to act. She spoke, and he nodded, and they talked a little bit, and it didn't look like she had ever seen him before. She drank out, and he let it ride for a minute, then he ordered another.

When I got it, what she was in there for, I tried to lose interest in her, but my eyes kept coming back to her. After a few minutes, I knew she felt me there, and I knew some of the other tables had tumbled to what was going on. She kept pulling her *rebozo* around her, like it was cold, and hunching one shoulder up, so she half had her back to me. All that did was throw her head up still higher, and I couldn't take my eyes off her at all. So of course a bull-fighter is like any other ham, he's watching every table but his own, and he had no more sense than to see these looks that were going round. You understand, it's a dead-pan place, a big café with a lot of mugs sitting around with their hats on the back of their heads, eating, drinking, smoking, reading, and jabbering Spanish, and there wasn't any nudging, pointing, or hey-get-a-load-of-this. They strictly minded their business. Just the same, there would be a pair of eyes behind a newspaper that weren't on the newspaper, or maybe a waitress would stop by somebody, and say something, and there'd be a laugh just a little louder than a waitress's gag is generally worth. He sat there, with a kind of a foolish look on his face, snapping his fingernail against his glass, and then I felt a prickle go up my spine. He was getting up, he was coming over.

A guy with three pesos in his pocket doesn't want any trouble, and when the room froze like a stop-camera shot, I tried to tell myself to play it friendly, to get out of it without starting something I couldn't stop. But when he stood there in front of me he still had on that hat.

"My table, he interest you, ha?"

"Your—what?"

"My table. You look, you seem interest, Señor."

"Oh, now I understand."

I wasn't playing it friendly, I was playing it mean. I got up, with the best smile I could paste on my face, and waved at a chair. "Of course. I shall explain. I shall gladly explain." Down there you make it simple, because spig reception isn't any too good. "Please sit down."

He looked at me and he looked at the chair, but it looked like he had me on the run, so he sat down. I sat down. Then I did something I wanted to do for fifteen minutes. I lifted that cream hat off his head, like it was the nicest thing I knew to do for him, slipped a menu card under it, and put it on a chair. If he had moved I was going to let him have it, if they shot me for it. He didn't. It caught him by surprise. A buzz went over the room. The first round was mine.

"May I order you something, Señor?"

He blinked, and I don't think he even heard me. Then he began looking around for help. He was used to having a gallery yell *Olé* every time he wiped his nose, but it had walked out on him this time. It was all deadpan, what he saw, and so far as they were concerned, we weren't even there. There wasn't anything he could do but face me, and try to remember what he had come for.

"The explain. Begin, please."

I had caught him with one he wasn't looking for, and I decided to let him have another, right between the eyes. "Certainly. I did look, that is true. But not at you. Believe me, Señor, not at you. And not at the table. At the lady."

". . . You—tell me this? You tell me this thing?"

"Sure. Why not?"

Well, what was he going to do? He could challenge me to a duel, but they never heard of a duel in Mexico. He could take a poke at me, but I outweighed him by about fifty pounds. He could shoot me, but he didn't have any gun. I had broken all the rules. You're not supposed to talk like that in Mexico, and once you hand a Mexican something he never heard of, it takes him about a year to figure out the answer. He sat there blinking at me, and the red kept creeping over his ears and cheeks, and I gave him plenty of time to think of something, if he could, before I went on. "I tell you what, Señor. I have examined this lady with care, and I find her very lovely. I admire your taste. I envy your fortune. So let us put her in a lottery, and the lucky man wins. We'll each buy her a ticket, and the one holding the highest number buys her next drink. Yes?"

"I am constantly worried that the reader won't keep reading," said author Cain, "and I write every page with that in mind."

Cain was a master of techniques designed to keep the reader turning those pages. Also his chapter endings are models guaranteed to make one feel obligated to read on—some action is left unresolved, some important scene is promised in the next chapter, *something* is about to happen!

Charlotte Brontë, the eldest of the three writing Brontë sisters, published her one enduring novel, *Jane Eyre*, in 1847. It is the story, very unconventional for its time, of a shy, plain governess who ends up with her patron, Rochester, a violent and moody enigma.

Here is the first meeting of the two, who will end up happily married and parents at the end of the tumultuous novel (unlike Heathcliff and Cathy Earnshaw in sister Emily's gloomy *Wuthering Heights*):

The din was on the causeway: a horse was coming; the windings of the lane yet hid it, but it approached. I was just leaving the stile; yet, as the path was narrow, I sat still to let it go by. In those days I was young, and all sorts of fancies bright and dark tenanted my mind: the memories of nursery stories were there amongst other rubbish; and when they recurred, maturing youth added to them a vigour and vividness beyond what childhood could give. As this horse approached, and as I watched for it to appear through the dusk, I remembered certain of Bessie's tales, wherein figured a North-of-England spirit called a "Gytrash," which, in the form of horse, mule, or large dog, haunted solitary ways, and sometimes came upon belated travellers, as this horse was now coming upon me.

It was very near, but not yet in sight; when, in addition to the tramp, tramp, I heard a rush under the hedge, and close down by the hazel stems glided a great dog, whose black and white colour made him a distinct object against the trees. It was exactly one form of Bessie's Gytrash—a lion-like creature with long hair and a huge head: it passed me, however, quietly enough; not staying to look up, with strange pretercanine eyes, in my face, as I half expected it would. The horse followed,—a tall steed, and on its back a rider. The man, the human being, broke the spell at once. Nothing ever rode the Gytrash: it was always alone; and goblins, to my notions, though they might tenant the dumb carcasses of beasts, could scarce covet shelter in the commonplace human form. No Gytrash was this,—only a traveller taking the short cut to Millcote. He passed, and I went on; a few steps, and I turned: a sliding sound and an exclamation of "What the deuce is to do now?" and a clattering tumble, arrested my attention. Man and horse were down; they had slipped on the sheet of ice which glazed the causeway. The dog came bounding back, and seeing his master in a predicament, and hearing the horse groan, barked till the evening hills echoed the sound, which was deep in proportion to his magnitude. He snuffed round the prostrate group, and then he ran up to me; it was all he could do,—there was no other help at hand to summon. I obeyed him, and walked down to the traveller, by this time struggling himself free of his steed. His efforts were so vigorous, I thought he could not be much hurt; but I asked him the question—

"Are you injured, sir?"

I think he was swearing, but am not certain; however, he was pronouncing some formula which prevented him from replying to me directly.

"Can I do anything?" I asked again.

"You must just stand on one side," he answered as he rose, first to his knees, and then to his feet. I did; whereupon began a heaving, stamping, clattering process, accompanied by a barking and baying which removed me effectually some yards' distance; but I would not be driven quite away till I saw the event. This was finally fortunate; the horse was re-established, and the dog was silenced with a "Down, Pilot!" The traveller now, stooping, felt his foot and leg, as if trying whether they were sound; apparently something ailed them, for he halted to the stile whence I had just risen, and sat down.

I was in the mood for being useful, or at least officious, I think, for I now drew near him again.

"If you are hurt, and want help, sir, I can fetch some one either from Thornfield Hall or from Hay."

"Thank you: I shall do: I have no broken bones,—only a sprain"; and again he stood up and tried his foot, but the result extorted an involuntary "Ugh!"

Something of daylight still lingered, and the moon was waxing bright: I could see him plainly. His figure was enveloped in a riding cloak, fur collared and steel clasped; its details were not apparent, but I traced the general points of middle height and considerable breadth of chest. He had a dark face, with stern features and a heavy brow; his eyes and gathered eyebrows looked ireful and thwarted just now; he was past youth, but had not reached middle-age; perhaps he might be thirty-five. I felt no fear of him, and but little shyness. Had he been a handsome, heroic-looking young gentleman, I should not have dared to stand thus questioning him against his will, and offering my services unasked. I had hardly ever seen a handsome youth; never in my life spoken to one. I had a theoretical reverence and homage for beauty, elegance, gallantry, fascination; but had I met those qualities incarnate in masculine shape, I should have known instinctively that they neither had nor could have sympathy with anything in me, and should have shunned them as one would fire, lightning, or anything else that is bright but antipathetic.

If even this stranger had smiled and been good-humoured to me when I addressed him; if he had put off my offer of assistance gaily and with thanks, I should have gone on my way and not felt any vocation to renew inquiries: but the frown, the roughness of the traveller, set me at my ease: I retained my station when he waved to me to go, and announced—

"I cannot think of leaving you, sir, at so late an hour, in this solitary lane, till I see you are fit to mount your horse."

He looked at me when I said this; he had hardly turned his eyes in my direction before.

"I should think you ought to be at home yourself," said he, "if you have a home in this neighbourhood: where do you come from?"

"From just below; and I am not at all afraid of being out late when it is moonlight: I will run over to Hay for you with pleasure, if you wish it: indeed, I am going there to post a letter."

"You live just below—do you mean at that house with the battlements?" pointing to Thornfield Hall, on which the moon cast a hoary gleam, bringing it out distinct and pale from the woods, that, by contrast with the western sky, now seemed one mass of shadow.

"Yes, sir."

"Whose house is it?"

"Mr. Rochester's."

"Do you know Mr. Rochester?"

"No, I have never seen him."

"He is not resident, then?"

"No."

"Can you tell me where he is?"

"I cannot."

"You are not a servant at the hall, of course. You are—" He stopped, ran his eye over my dress, which, as usual, was quite simple: a black merino cloak, a black beaver bonnet; neither of them half fine enough for a lady's-maid. He seemed puzzled to decide what I was; I helped him.

"I am the governess."

"Ah, the governess!" he repeated; "deuce take me, if I had not forgotten! The governess!" and again my raiment underwent scrutiny. In two minutes he rose from the stile: his face expressed pain when he tried to move.

"I cannot commission you to fetch help," he said; "but you may help me a little yourself, if you will be so kind."

"Yes, sir."

"You have not an umbrella that I can use as a stick?"

"No."

"Try to get hold of my horse's bridle and lead him to me: you are not afraid?"

I should have been afraid to touch a horse when alone, but when told to do it, I was disposed to obey. I put down my muff on the stile, and went up to the tall steed; I endeavoured to catch the bridle, but it was a spirited thing, and would not let me come near its head; I made effort on effort, though in vain: meantime, I was mortally afraid of its trampling forefeet. The traveller waited and watched for some time, and at last he laughed.

"I see," he said, "the mountain will never be brought to Mahomet, so all you can do is to aid Mahomet to go to the mountain; I must beg of you to come here."

I came. "Excuse me," he continued: "necessity compels me to make you useful." He laid a heavy hand on my shoulder, and leaning on me with some stress, limped to his horse. Having once caught the bridle, he mastered it directly and sprang to his saddle; grimacing grimly as he made the effort, for it wrenched his sprain.

"Now," said he, releasing his under lip from a hard bite, "just hand me my whip; it lies there under the hedge."

I sought it and found it.

"Thank you; now make haste with the letter to Hay, and return as fast as you can."

A touch of a spurred heel made his horse first start and rear, and then bound away; the dog rushed in his traces; all three vanished.

"Like heath that, in the wilderness,
The wild wind whirls away."

I took up my muff and walked on. The incident had occurred and was gone for me: it *was* an incident of no moment, no romance, no interest in a sense; yet it marked with change one single hour of a monotonous life. My help had been needed and claimed; I had given it: I was pleased to have done something; trivial, transitory though the deed was, it was yet an active thing, and I was weary of an existence all passive. The new face, too, was like a new picture introduced to the gallery of memory; and it was dissimilar to all the others hanging there: firstly, because it was masculine; and, secondly, because it was dark, strong, and stern. I had it still before me when I entered Hay, and slipped the letter into the post-office; I saw it as I walked fast down-hill all the way home.

Notice how Jane avers that there is "no romance" in the incident.

Hah! *We* know better, don't we?

One always has an intriguing situation when two people are thrown together by circumstances and come to love each other, but, though the readers know it, they don't. I always liked the line in the film *Easter Parade* when Fred Astaire, starry-eyed after watching Judy Garland sing, says to her reproachfully and tenderly: "Why didn't you *tell* me I was in love with you?"

When a man and a woman who are to become lovers at a later date meet in somewhat adversarial attitude or situation, it seems to heighten our interest and expectation.

With that in mind, go to your library and read the following diverse encounters of lovers:

Dick Diver and Nicole in *Tender Is the Night*, F. Scott Fitzgerald

Vronsky and Anna in *Anna Karenina*, Leo Tolstoy

Scarlett and Rhett in *Gone with the Wind*, Margaret
Mitchell

Elizabeth and Darcy in *Pride and Prejudice*, Jane
Austen

And, for fun:

Jane and Lord Greystoke, aka Tarzan, in *Tarzan of the
Apes*, Edgar Rice Burroughs

CHAPTER SEVEN

ACTION

All through this book we've emphasized Scott Fitzgerald's maxim "Action is character."

And, of course, it is true. Even the way someone drinks his or her tea can be termed an action and can be at the same time revealing of character. (Does the truck driver drink it with his pinkie extended? Does the dowager gulp it and slosh it around in her mouth before swallowing? Does the accused murderer enfold both hands around the Dresden cup and take delicate sips with pursed lips?)

But what we generally mean when we speak of "action" in stories is of a more physical type—a narration of a dramatic, exciting, and often dangerous happening or happenings.

Graham Greene has written spiritual books and pure adventure books, but in all his writings he has what could be described as action scenes.

In his autobiography, *A Sort of Life*, Greene summed up the writing of action, or what he calls "excitement," better than anything else I've read:

Excitement is simple: excitement is a situation, a single event. It mustn't be wrapped up in thoughts, similes, metaphors. A simile is a form of reflection, but excitement is of the moment when there is no time to reflect. Action can only be expressed by a subject, a verb, and an object, perhaps a rhythm—little else. Even an adjective slows the pace or tranquilizes the nerve. I should have turned to Stevenson to learn my lesson:

> It came all of a sudden when it did, with a rush of feet and a roar, and then a shout from Alan, and the sound of blows and someone crying as if hurt. I looked back over my shoulder and saw Mr. Shuan in the doorway crossing blades with Alan.

No similes or metaphors there, not even an adjective. But I was too concerned with "the point of view" to be aware of simpler problems, to know that the sort of novel I was trying to write, unlike a poem, was not made with words but with movement, action, character. Discrimination in one's word is certainly required, but not love of one's words. . . .

It is worth reading this passage of Greene's several times.

As to the subject of the adjective, remember Mark Twain's admonition "when in doubt, strike it out."

Movement, action, character. . . .

Graham Greene follows his own admonitions and advice in this beginning of his action-packed novel *A Gun for Sale* (published in America as *This Gun for Hire*):

> Murder didn't mean much to Raven. It was just a new job. You had to be careful. You had to use your brains. It was not a question of hatred. He had only seen the Minister once: he had been pointed out to Raven as he walked down the new housing estate between the small lit Christmas

trees, an old grubby man without friends, who was said to love humanity.

The cold wind cut Raven's face in the wide Continental street. It was a good excuse for turning the collar of his coat well above his mouth. A hare-lip was a serious handicap in his profession; it had been badly sewn in infancy, so that now the upper lip was twisted and scarred. When you carried about so easy an identification you couldn't help becoming ruthless in your methods. It had always, from the first, been necessary for Raven to eliminate a witness.

He carried an attaché case. He looked like any other youngish man going home after his work; his dark overcoat had a clerical air. He moved steadily up the street like hundreds of his kind. A tram went by, lit up in the early dusk: he didn't take it. An economical young man, you might have thought, saving money for his home. Perhaps even now he was on his way to meet his girl.

But Raven had never had a girl. The hare-lip prevented that. He had learnt, when he was very young, how repulsive it was. He turned into one of the tall grey houses and climbed the stairs, a sour bitter screwed-up figure.

Outside the top flat he put down his attaché case and put on gloves. He took a pair of clippers out of his pocket and cut through the telephone wire where it ran out from above the door to the lift shaft. Then he rang the bell.

He hoped to find the Minister alone. This little top-floor flat was the socialist's home; he lived in a poor bare solitary way and Raven had been told that his secretary always left him at half-past six; he was very considerate with his employees. But Raven was a minute too early and the Minister half an hour too late. A woman opened the door, an elderly woman with pince-nez and several gold teeth. She had her hat on and her coat was over her arm. She had been on the point of leaving and she was furious at being caught. She didn't allow him to speak, but snapped at him in German, "The Minister is engaged."

He wanted to spare her, not because he minded a killing but because his employers would prefer him not to exceed his instructions. He held the letter of introduction out to her silently; as long as she didn't hear his foreign voice or see the hare-lip she was safe. She took the letter primly and held it up close to her pince-nez. Good, he thought, she's short-sighted. "Stay where you are," she said, and walked back up the passage. He could hear her disapproving governess voice, then she was back in the passage saying, "The Minister will see you. Follow me, please." He couldn't understand the foreign speech, but he knew what she meant from her behaviour.

His eyes, like little concealed cameras, photographed the room instantaneously: the desk, the easy chair, the map on the wall, the door to the bedroom behind, the wide window above the bright cold Christmas street. A small oil-stove was all the heating, and the Minister was having it used now to boil a saucepan. A kitchen alarm-clock on the desk marked seven o'clock. A voice said, "Emma, put in another egg." The Minister came out from the bedroom. He had tried to tidy himself, but he had forgotten the cigarette ash on his trousers, and his fingers were ink-stained. The secretary took an egg out of one of the drawers in the desk. "And the salt. Don't forget the salt," the Minister said. He explained in slow English, "It prevents the shell cracking. Sit down, my friend. Make yourself at home. Emma, you can go."

Raven sat down and fixed his eyes on the Minister's chest. He thought: I'll give her three minutes by the alarm-clock to get well away: he kept his eyes on the Minister's chest: just there I'll shoot. He let his coat collar fall and saw with bitter rage how the old man turned away from the sight of his hare-lip.

The Minister said, "It's years since I heard from him. But I've never forgotten him, never. I can show you his photograph in the other room. It's good of him to think of an old friend. So rich and powerful too. You must ask him when you go back if he remembers the time—" A bell began to ring furiously.

Raven thought: the telephone. I cut the wire. It shook his nerve. But it was only the alarm-clock drumming on the desk. The Minister turned it off. "One egg's boiled," he said and stooped for the saucepan. Raven opened his attaché case: in the lid he had fixed his automatic fitted with a silencer. The Minister said: "I'm sorry the bell made you jump. You see I like my egg just four minutes."

Feet ran along the passage. The door opened. Raven turned furiously in his seat, his hare-lip flushed and raw. It was the secretary. He thought: my God, what a household. They won't let a man do things tidily. He forgot his lip, he was angry, he had a grievance. She came in flashing her gold teeth, prim and ingratiating. She said, "I was just going out when I heard the telephone," then she winced slightly, looked the other way, showed a clumsy delicacy before his deformity which he couldn't help noticing. It condemned her. He snatched the automatic out of the case and shot the Minister twice in the back.

The Minister fell across the oil-stove; the saucepan upset and the two eggs broke on the floor. Raven shot the Minister once more in the head, leaning across the desk to make quite certain, driving the bullet hard into the base of the skull, smashing it open like a china doll's. Then he turned on the secretary; she moaned at him; she hadn't any words; the old mouth couldn't hold its saliva. He supposed she was begging him for mercy. He pressed the trigger again; she staggered under it as if she had been kicked by an animal in the side. But he had miscalculated. Her unfashionable dress, the swathes of useless material in which she hid her body, had perhaps confused his aim. And she was tough, so tough he couldn't believe his eyes; she was through the door before he could fire again, slamming it behind her.

But she couldn't lock it; the key was on his side. He twisted the handle and pushed; the elderly woman had amazing strength; it only gave two inches. She began to scream some word at the top of her voice.

There was no time to waste. He stood away from the door and shot twice through the woodwork. He could hear the pince-nez fall on the floor and break. The voice screamed again and stopped; there was a sound outside as if she were sobbing. It was her breath going out through her wounds. Raven was satisfied. . . .

It was time to be gone. He took the automatic with him.

Movement, action, character.
What wonderful details, what terse and vivid sentences:

He could hear the prince-nez fall on the floor and break.

How chilling the simple sentence:

It condemned her.

Notice how Graham Greene never lets us forget Raven's harelip and its effect on himself and other people; Greene never puts pure action ahead of character development.

I frequently see beginning writers start their stories with action, often violent action, often well described, and yet we are not grabbed, not lured into the story, not moved. Why?

The veteran film director Budd Boetticher tells of a famous producer invited to view the first rushes of a new film. In the screening room the lights went down and on the screen one saw a speeding car appear at the top of a steep hill. The automobile careened and screeched around one curve after another and finally hurtled off the edge of a cliff to crash and explode on the rocks 200 feet below.

The lights in the room came on, and someone exclaimed: "Isn't that the greatest opening of a film ever?"

The producer puffed on a cigar for a moment and then asked: "Who's in the car?"

Before you start any plotty stuff with your story, any great dialogue, or any spectacular action, ask yourself one vital question: *Who's in the car?*

With Graham Greene we always know—and care—who's in the car.

Here is a good nonfiction example of an action story beginning. It comes from *The Capture of Adolf Eichmann* by Bela W. von Block:

The tall, gaunt man with protruding ears and a receding hairline got off the bus and started to walk along the murky Buenos Aires street. Outwardly he was relaxed, just another working man after a hard day. Inwardly he was tense, watchful—as he had been, day and night, for fifteen years.

He saw nothing to cause him alarm. In the middle of the block a tramp squatted on a discarded crate. Fifty feet beyond, two housewives stood gossiping. Farther along, two day laborers were lighting cigarettes. A dark, nondescript sedan turned into the street. The jug-eared man saw it coming and edged instinctively toward the buildings on his left. The sedan drew closer, braked to a sudden halt. The doors were flung open, and four men leaped out. He tried to run, but it was useless. He was surrounded.

"Guten Abend, Herr Obersturmbannführer!"

He heard the snarled words and opened his mouth to scream, but something struck him a crushing blow on the head. He slumped, and strong hands thrust his unconscious body into the waiting car. The four men piled into the sedan; the driver blinked his headlights twice, then drove away.

The great manhunt was over. Adolf Eichmann—the man who had often boasted that he was the "World's No. 1 Jew-Killer"—had been taken prisoner by the people he hated most, the people who had tracked him relentlessly for a decade and a half.

Terse, explicit, swift, and involving. *Who, what, when, why, where.* And we know very well who is in—in this case—the sedan.

C. S. Forester wrote splendid action novels. His accounts of naval encounters in his acclaimed Hornblower series are models of historical fiction.

But he didn't always write about adventures of epic proportions. His short novel, *The African Queen*, written in 1935, tells of the unlikely hegira of an unlikely couple, spinster Rose Sayer and the not-too-bright cockney Charlie Allnutt. It is World War I and, due to the death of her missionary brother, Rose is forced to flee the Germans in the heart of Africa by going down the length of the Ulanga River in Allnutt's ancient launch, the *African Queen*. After many vividly described adventures they come to Lake Wittelsbach and they decide to strike a blow for England. They will blow up the gunship *Königin Luise* which has control of the big lake. They have fallen in love, and here we are close to the end:

Allnutt and Rose watched the *Königin Luise* come back from her excursion to the south, and they saw her head over towards the islands, and, as the day was waning, they saw her come to a stop at the point where she had anchored before. Both their hearts were beating faster. It was then that the question they had debated in academic fashion a week earlier without reaching a satisfactory conclusion solved itself. They had just turned away from looking at the *Königin Luise*, about to make preparations to start, when they found themselves holding each other's hands and looking into each other's eyes. Each of them knew what was in the other's mind.

"Rosie, old girl," said Allnutt, hoarsely. "We're going out *together*, aren't we?"

Rose nodded.

"Yes, dear," she said. "I should like it that way."

Confronted with the sternest need for a decision, she had reached it without difficulty. They would share all the dangers, and stand the same chance, side by side, when the *African Queen* drove her torpedoes smashing against the side of the *Königin Luise*. They could not endure the thought of being parted, now. They could even smile at the prospect of going into eternity together.

It was almost dark by now. The young moon was low in the sky; soon there would only be the stars to give them light.

"It's safe for us to get ready now," said Rose. "Goodbye, dear."

"Goodbye darling, sweet'eart," said Allnutt.

Their preparations took much time, as they had anticipated. They had all night before them, and they knew that as it was a question of surprise the best time they could reach the *Königin Luise* would be in the early hours of the morning. Allnutt had to go down into the mud and water and cut away the reeds about the *African Queen*'s stern before they could slide her out into the channel again—the reeds which had parted before her bows resisted obstinately the passage of her stern and propeller.

When they were in the river, moored lightly to a great bundle of reeds, Allnutt quietly took the detonators from the locker and went into the water again over the bows. He was a long time there, standing in mud and deep water while he screwed the detonators home into the noses of the cylinders. The rough-and-ready screw threads he had scratched in the edges of his discs did not enter kindly into their functions. Allnutt had to use force, and it was a slow process to use force in the dark on a detonator in contact with a hundred-weight of high explosive. Rose stood in the bows to help him at need as he worked patiently at the task. If his hand should slip against those nail-heads they would be blown into fragments, and the *Königin Luise* would still rule the waves of the Lake.

Nor did the fact that the *African Queen* was pitching a little in a slight swell coming in from the lake help Allnutt at all in his task, but he finished it in the end. In the almost pitch dark, Rose saw him back away from the torpedoes and come round at a safe distance to the side of the boat. His hands reached up and he swung himself on board, dripping.

"Done it," he whispered—they could not help whispering in that darkness with the obsession of their future errand upon them.

Allnutt groped about the boat putting up the funnel again. He made a faint noise with his spanner as he tightened up the nuts on the funnel stay bolts. It all took time.

The furnace was already charged with fuel—that much, at any rate, they had been able to make ready days ago— and the tin canister of matches was in its right place, and he could light the dry friable stuff and close down to force the draught. He knew just whereabouts to lay his hands on the various sorts of wood he might need before they reached the *Königin Luise*.

There was a wind blowing now, and the *African Queen* was very definitely pitching to the motion of the water. The noise of the draught seemed loud to their anxious ears, and when Allnutt recharged the furnace a volley of sparks shot from the funnel and was swept away overhead. Rose had never seen sparks issue from that funnel before—she had only been in the *African Queen* under way in day-light—and she realized the danger that the sparks might reveal their approach. She spoke quietly to Allnutt about it.

"Can't 'elp it, Miss, sometimes," he whispered back. "I'll see it don't 'appen when we're getting close to 'em."

The engine was sighing and slobbering now; if it had been daylight they would have seen the steam oozing out of the leaky joints.

"S'ss, s'ss," whistled Allnutt, between his teeth.

"All right," said Rose.

Allnutt unfastened the side painter and took the boat hook. A good thrust against a clump of reeds sent the boat out into the fairway; he laid the boat hook down, and felt for the throttle valve and opened it. The propeller began its beat and the engine its muffled clanking. Rose stood at the tiller and steered out down the dark river mouth. They were off now, to strike their blow for the land of hope and glory of which Rose had sung as a child at concerts in Sunday school choirs. They were going to set wider those bounds and make the mighty country mightier yet.

All that for nought! The *African Queen* sinks!

But do not despair—they are rescued, and shortly thereafter the gunship is also sunk. And Rosie and Charlie get married for a happy ending.

In this book Forester proves that the fate of a thirty-foot rotting launch in an obscure lake in Africa can seem to be every bit as important to a reader as, say, Lord Nelson's flagship at Trafalgar, if the writer makes the characters likable and their problem believable and compelling.

John Huston made a faithful and popular film of this book starring Katherine Hepburn and Humphrey Bogart, and before Rosie and Charlie's watery ordeal was over we cared very much who was in the boat.

No one will dispute that Mark Twain was a master of action, whether it be concerned with a scene about a festive jumping frog contest or a scary episode with a murderous Indian in a cave or a life-saving eclipse of the sun in the time of King Arthur.

Huckleberry Finn is considered one of the bright gems in literature, and to many people it is the genesis of modern American writing: "All modern American literature comes from one book by Mark Twain called *Huckleberry Finn*," wrote Ernest Hemingway.

At the beginning of the novel Huck is living with his drunken brute of a father and, tired of the beatings, he plans to take off down the river in a canoe he has found and hidden. But how to cover his tracks so that he won't be followed and dragged back?

While we laid off after breakfast to sleep up, both of us being about wore out, I got to thinking that if I could fix up some way to keep pap and the widow from trying to follow me, it would be a certainer thing than trusting to luck to get far enough off before they missed me; you see, all kinds of things might happen. Well, I didn't see no way for a while, but by and by pap raised up a minute to drink another barrel of water, and he says:

"Another time a man comes a-prowling round here you roust me out, you hear? That man warn't here for no good. I'd a shot him. Next time you roust me out, you hear?"

Then he dropped down and went to sleep again; what he had been saying give me the very idea I wanted. I says to myself, I can fix it now so nobody won't think of following me.

About twelve o'clock we turned out and went along up the bank. The river was coming up pretty fast, and lots of driftwood going by on the rise. By and by along comes part of a log raft—nine logs fast together. We went out with the

skiff and towed it ashore. Then we had dinner. Anybody
but pap would 'a' waited and seen the day through, so as
to catch more stuff; but that warn't pap's style. Nine logs
was enough for one time; he must shove right over to town
and sell. So he locked me in and took the skiff, and started
off towing the raft about half-past three. I judged he
wouldn't come back that night. I waited till I reckoned he
had got a good start; then I out with my saw, and went to
work on that log again. Before he was t'other side of the
river I was out of the hole; him and his raft was just a
speck on the water away off yonder.

I took the sack of corn meal and took it to where the canoe was hid, and shoved the vines and branches apart and
put it in; then I done the same with the side of bacon; then
the whisky jug. I took all the coffee and sugar there was,
and all the ammunition; I took the wadding; I took the
bucket and gourd; took a dipper and a tin cup, and my old
saw and two blankets, and the skillet and the coffee-pot. I
took fish-lines and matches and other things—everything
that was worth a cent. I cleaned out the place. I wanted an
ax, but there wasn't any, only the one out at the woodpile,
and I knowed why I was going to leave that. I fetched out
the gun, and now I was done.

I had wore the ground a good deal crawling out of the
hole and dragging out so many things. So I fixed that as
good as I could from the outside by scattering dust on the
place, which covered up the smoothness and the sawdust.
Then I fixed the piece of log back into its place, and put
two rocks under it and one against it to hold it there, for it
was bent up at that place and didn't quite touch ground. If
you stood four or five foot away and didn't know it was
sawed, you wouldn't never notice it; and besides, this was
the back of the cabin, and it warn't likely anybody would
go fooling around there.

It was all grass clear to the canoe, so I hadn't left a

track. I followed around to see. I stood on the bank and looked out over the river. All safe. So I took the gun and went up a piece into the woods, and was hunting around for some birds when I see a wild pig; hogs soon went wild in them bottoms after they had got away from the prairie farms. I shot this fellow and took him into camp.

I took the ax and smashed in the door. I beat it and hacked it considerable a-doing it. I fetched the pig in, and took him back nearly to the table and hacked into his throat with the ax, and laid him down on the ground to bleed; I say ground because it *was* ground—hard packed, and no boards. Well, next I took an old sack and put a lot of big rocks in it—all I could drag—and I started it from the pig, and dragged it to the door and through the woods down to the river and dumped it in, and down it sunk, out of sight. You could easy see that something had been dragged over the ground. I did wish Tom Sawyer was there; I knowed he would take an interest in this kind of business and throw in the fancy touches. Nobody could spread himself like Tom Sawyer in such a thing as that.

Well, last I pulled out some of my hair, and blooded the ax good, and stuck it on the back side, and slung the ax in the corner. Then I took up the pig and held him to my breast with my jacket (so he couldn't drip) till I got a good piece below the house and then dumped him into the river. Now I thought of something else. So I went and got the bag of meal and my old saw out of the canoe, and fetched them to the house. I took the bag to where it used to stand, and ripped a hole in the bottom of it with the saw, for there warn't no knives and forks on the place—pap done everything with his clasp-knife about the cooking. Then I carried the sack about a hundred yards across the grass and through the willows east of the house, to a shallow lake that was five miles wide and full of rushes—and ducks too, you might say, in the season. There was a slough or a creek

leading out of it on the other side that went miles away, I
don't know where, but it didn't go to the river. The meal
sifted out and made a little track all the way to the lake. I
dropped pap's whetstone there too, so as to look like it had
been done by accident. Then I tied up the rip in the meal
sack with a string, so it wouldn't leak no more, and took it
and my saw to the canoe again.

It was about dark now; so I dropped the canoe down the
river under some willows that hung over the bank, and
waited for the moon to rise. I made fast to a willow; then
I took a bite to eat, and by and by laid down in the canoe
to smoke a pipe and lay out a plan. I says to myself, they'll
follow the track of that sackful of rocks to the shore and
then drag the river for me. And they'll follow that meal
track to the lake and go browsing down the creek that leads
out of it to find the robbers that killed me and took the
things. They won't ever hunt the river for anything but my
dead carcass. They'll soon get tired of that, and won't
bother no more about me. All right; I can stop anywhere I
want to. Jackson's Island is good enough for me; I know
that island pretty well, and nobody ever comes there. And
then I can paddle over to town nights, and slink around and
pick up things I want. Jackson's Island's the place.

I was pretty tired, and the first thing I knowed I was
asleep. When I woke up I didn't know where I was for a
minute. I set up and looked around, a little scared. Then I
remembered. The river looked miles and miles across. The
moon was so bright I could 'a' counted the drift logs that
went a-slipping along, black and still, hundreds of yards
out from shore. Everything was dead quiet, and it looked
late, and *smelled* late. You know what I mean—I don't
know the words to put it in.

I took a good gap and a stretch, and was just going to
unhitch and start when I heard a sound away over the water. Pretty soon I made it out. It was that dull kind of a reg-

ular sound that comes from oars working in rowlocks when it's a still night. I peeped out through the willow branches, and there it was—a skiff, away across the water. I couldn't tell how many was in it. It kept a-coming, and when it was abreast of me I see there warn't but one man in it. Thinks I, maybe it's pap, though I warn't expecting him. He dropped below me with the current, and by and by he came a-swinging up shore in the easy water, and he went by so close I could 'a' reached out the gun and touched him. Well, it *was* pap, sure enough—and sober, too, by the way he laid his oars.

I didn't lose no time. The next minute I was a-spinning downstream soft, but quick, in the shade of the bank.

That, I need not tell you, is good narrative writing. Notice how Twain doesn't just say that Huck "took some supplies" from the house—he *itemizes* them. We "see" each one.

Readers like details and specifics!

And we enjoy seeing every clever maneuver that the boy, Huck, thinks up to complete his phony murder scene. We always enjoy reading about clever people, resourceful people; not about people who are good at nothing, who can't cope— wimps. We become *involved* with Huck—
Why?
First, because he is likable and because he has a big problem, one we can identify with: How terrible to be forced to live with a drunken, abusive, perhaps dangerous, parent.
Secondly, he is doing something about his problem, rather than just whining about it passively.
Twain knew how to depict action and he knew how to tell a story. We should never lose sight of the fact that we writers are first and foremost storytellers.

In his 1927 *Aspects of the Novel*, E. M. Forster says somewhat diffidently, ambivalently, and very English in tone:

> Yes—oh, dear, yes—the novel tells a story. . . . That is the highest factor common to all novels, and I wish that it was not so, that it could be something different—melody, or perception of the truth, not this low atavistic form.

Low or not, everyone has loved a good story since time immemorial and in that sense the novel is certainly atavistic.

Many action stories and novels end in death, violent or otherwise. One would expect death in a book entitled *War and Peace* and Count Leo Tolstoy does not disappoint us. Here is the action scene where Prince Andrei is fatally wounded at the Battle of Borodino:

> Another time general attention was attracted by a small brown dog—which had appeared from heaven knows where—busily trotting along in front of the regiment with its tail erect, till suddenly a cannonball fell close by and it darted off with a yelp, its tail between its legs. Howls and shrieks of laughter rose from the whole regiment. But distractions of this kind lasted only a few minutes, and the pale and sullen faces of these men, who for eight hours had been inactive, without food, and in constant fear of death, kept growing paler and more sullen.
>
> Prince Andrei, pale and depressed like everyone else in the regiment, paced up and down from one border to another in the meadow next to the oat field, his head bowed, his hands clasped behind his back. There were no orders to be given, nothing for him to do. Everything happened of itself. The dead were dragged back from the front, the wounded carried away, and again the ranks closed up. If any soldier ran to the rear, he made haste to return at once.

At first Prince Andrei, considering it his duty to keep up the spirits of his men and to set them an example, had walked about among the ranks, but he was soon convinced that this served no purpose, that there was nothing they could learn from him. All the powers of his soul, like those of every soldier there, were unconsciously directed to keeping his mind off the horrors of their situation. He walked along the meadow, dragging his feet, rustling the grass, and contemplating the dust that covered his boots; then he took long strides, trying to step on the tracks left by the mowers; then counted his steps, calculating how many times he would have to walk from one border to another to make a verst; then stripped the flowers from the wormwood growing along the edge of the field, rubbed them between his palms and inhaled their pungent, bittersweet aroma. Nothing remained of the previous day's thoughts. He was thinking of nothing at all. He listened with ears that had grown weary of the same sounds, distinguishing the hiss of flying projectiles and cannon reports, and glanced at the tiresomely familiar faces of the men in the first battalion. . . . "Here it comes . . . this one's for us!" he thought, hearing the approaching whistle of something flying out of that smoke-filled region. "One! Another! Still another! . . . A hit . . ." he stopped and looked along the ranks. "No, it's gone over. . . . But that one hit!" And he resumed his pacing up and down, trying to take long strides to reach the border in sixteen paces.

A hiss and a thud! Five paces from him a cannonball tore up the dry earth and vanished. A chill ran down his spine. Again he glanced at the ranks. Probably many had been blown up; a large crowd had gathered near the second battalion.

"Adjutant!" he shouted. "Order them not to crowd together."

The adjutant, having obeyed the order, approached

Prince Andrei. The battalion commander rode up from the other side.

"Look out!" cried a soldier in a terrified voice, and like a bird in swift flight coming to earth with a whirr of wings, a shell landed almost noiselessly two paces from Prince Andrei.

The horse, not having to question whether it was right or wrong to show fear, was the first to react, snorting, rearing, and almost throwing the major as it sprang to one side. The horse's terror was communicated to the men.

"Lie down!" shouted the adjutant, throwing himself to the ground.

Prince Andrei hesitated. The smoking shell, which had fallen near a clump of wormwood on the border of the plowed field and the meadow, spun like a top between him and the prostrate adjutant.

"Can this be death?" thought Prince Andrei, looking with unwonted yearning at the grass, the wormwood, and then at the wisp of smoke curling up from the rotating black ball. "I can't die, I don't want to die. I love life—love this grass, this earth, this air . . ."

Even while he was thinking these thoughts, he remembered that people were looking at him.

"It's shameful, sir!" he said to the adjutant. "What kind of——"

He did not finish. There was the sound of an explosion, like the splintering of a window frame being ripped out, and at the same moment, a suffocating smell of powder, and Prince Andrei was hurled to one side, and flinging up his arm fell face downward.

Several officers ran up to him. Blood poured from the right side of his abdomen, making a great stain on the grass.

The militiamen with stretchers, who had been summoned, stood behind the officers. Prince Andrei lay flat on his chest, his face in the grass, breathing in hoarse gasps.

"Well, what are you waiting for? Come along!"

The peasants took Prince Andrei by the legs and shoulders, but he moaned piteously, and the men exchanged glances and set him down again.

"Pick him up, get him on there anyhow!" someone shouted.

Once more they lifted him by the shoulders and laid him on the stretcher.

"Oh, my God, my God! . . . What is it? . . . In the belly? . . . He's done for! . . . Oh, my God!" the officers were heard exclaiming.

"It whizzed right past my ear—just grazed it!" said the adjutant.

The peasants, adjusting the stretcher to their shoulders, hastily set off along the path they had trodden to the dressing station.

"Keep in step! . . . Ah, these peasants!" cried an officer, putting his hand on the shoulder of one of the men to check the uneven pace that was jolting the stretcher.

"Keep in step, Fyodor! Hey, Fyodor!" said the foremost peasant.

"That's it, I've got it now," said the one behind, delighted that he had fallen into step.

"Your Excellency! Ah! Prince!" said Timokhin in a trembling voice, having run up and looked down at the stretcher.

Prince Andrei opened his eyes and looked up at the speaker from the depths of the stretcher into which his head was sunk, and his eyelids drooped again.

The militiamen carried Prince Andrei to a dressing station near a wood. The dressing station consisted of three tents with their flaps tied back, which had been pitched at the edge of a birch wood. The horses and berlins stood among the trees. The horses were feeding, and sparrows flew down to pick up the grains that fell from their feed bags. The crows, scenting blood, were flying about in the trees, cawing clamorously. Over an area of more than five versts around the tents, bloodstained men, variously attired, stood, sat, or lay. Crowds of stretcher-bearers, whom the officers maintaining order tried in vain to disperse, stood about, dolefully gazing at them. Paying no heed to the officers, these men leaned on their stretchers, staring intently before them, as if trying to grasp the perplexing significance of the spectacle they were witnessing. From the tents came loud frantic cries mingled with plaintive moans. At intervals, a doctor's assistant ran out for water or to point out those who were to be brought in next. The wounded men, awaiting their turn outside the tents, cried out in raucous voices, groaned, wept, screamed, swore, begged for vodka. Some were delirious.

Prince Andrei's bearers, stepping over the wounded who had not yet been attended to, carried him, as a regimental commander, close to one of the tents, where they stopped and waited for instructions. Prince Andrei opened his eyes, but for a long time was unable to make out what was going on around him. He remembered the meadow, the clump of wormwood, the plowed field, the whirling black ball, and his sudden, passionate surge of love for life.

A couple of paces from him, leaning on the branch of a tree and attracting general attention with his loud talk, stood a tall, handsome, black-haired noncommissioned officer with a bandaged head. He had bullet wounds in both his head and his leg. A crowd of wounded men and stretcher-bearers were gathered around him, eagerly listening to what he said.

"We battered away at him till he chucked everything—we caught the king himself," he said, looking about with black eyes that glittered feverishly. "If only the reserves had come up just then, believe me, lads, there wouldn't have been nothing left of him."

Like all the others near the speaker, Prince Andrei looked at him with shining eyes, feeling a sense of comfort.

"But isn't it all the same now?" he thought. "And what will it be like there . . . and what has it been here? Why was I so reluctant to relinquish life? There was something about this life that I did not and do not now understand."

Now, if you have only heard of but not read any of *War and Peace* before, you can see from this typical excerpt that there is nothing intimidating about it. Just because many critics have called the work "the greatest novel ever written" does not mean it is hard to read. There is nothing difficult about the book—except its great length. So, instead of reading four inferior current best-sellers, why not apply yourself to reading this milestone in world literature?

Sadly, every story, if carried far enough, will end in death, and many many great writers have ended their novels with that most final of actions. For example, Evelyn Waugh treated death solemnly and splendidly in *Brideshead Revisited* and *A Handful of Dust*; and satirically and splendidly in *Scoop* and *The Loved One*.

Nearly all of Hemingway's novels end with the demise of the protagonist, and most of that writer's best short stories do likewise.

In a similar manner most of Joseph Conrad's action-filled stories and novels end in violence and death. In Conrad's 1915 exotic romance set in the East Indies, *Victory*, Axel Heyst has escaped from life's turmoil by retreating to the tropical island of Samburan. He falls in love with a young woman, Lena, from a touring group of entertainers performing in Sourabaya and takes her back to his island. They live in happiness until the arrival of three evil men—Jones,

Ricardo, and Pedro—looking for the treasure Heyst is ru-
mored to have. The Chinese servant has fled with Heyst's pis-
tol, and he and Lena are helpless. Then, to protect the man
she loves, Lena seduces Ricardo to gain possession of his
knife. When Heyst and Jones enter the bungalow and see
Lena and Ricardo, Jones fires at his erstwhile partner in
crime. He misses but hits Lena by mistake:

    The faint smile on her deep-cut lips waned, and her head
sank deep into the pillow, taking on the majestic pallor and
immobility of marble. But over the muscles, which seemed
set in their transfigured beauty for ever, passed a slight and
awful tremor. With an amazing strength she asked loudly:
    "What's the matter with me?"
    "You have been shot, dear Lena," Heyst said in a steady
voice, while Davidson, at the question, turned away and
leaned his forehead against the post of the foot of the bed.
    "Shot? I did think, too, that something had struck me."
    Over Samburan the thunder had ceased to growl at last,
and the world of material forms shuddered no more under
the emerging stars. The spirit of the girl which was passing
away from under them clung to her triumph convinced of
the reality of her victory over death.
    "No more," she muttered. "There will be no more! Oh,
my beloved," she cried weakly, "I've saved you! Why don't
you take me into your arms and carry me out of this lonely
place?"
    Heyst bent low over her, cursing his fastidious soul,
which even at that moment kept the true cry of love from
his lips in its infernal mistrust of all life. He dared not
touch her, and she had no longer the strength to throw her
arms about his neck.
    "Who else could have done this for you?" she whispered
gloriously.

"No one in the world," he answered her in a murmur of unconcealed despair.

She tried to raise herself, but all she could do was to lift her head a little from the pillow. With a terrified and gentle movement, Heyst hastened to slip his arm under her neck. She felt relieved at once of an intolerable weight, and was content to surrender to him the infinite weariness of her tremendous achievement. Exulting, she saw herself extended on the bed, in a black dress, and profoundly at peace; while, stooping over her with a kindly, playful smile, he was ready to lift her up in his firm arms and take her into the sanctuary of his innermost heart—for ever! The flush of rapture flooding her whole being broke out in a smile of innocent, girlish happiness; and with that divine radiance on her lips she breathed her last, triumphant, seeking for his glance in the shades of death.

This is a romantic, sentimental, and accessible Joseph Conrad that he keeps well hidden in most of his other writings.

Exulting, she saw herself extended on the bed, in a black dress, and profoundly at peace. . . .

brings to mind Freud's potent observation: "No man can believe in his own death, and when he tries to imagine it, he perceives that he really survives as a spectator."

Strange, I can think of few memorable birthing scenes in literature; David Copperfield and his caul and Prissy's "I don' know nuffin 'bout birthin', Miss Scarlett" come to mind, and that's about all. Yet there are a plethora of death scenes.

When I was sixteen, William Saroyan was brought home to our house from a bar by my older brother for what became a wild weekend. I was told that "Bill" was a "promising writer," and he himself told me he'd just written "a story that will make me world-famous."

It did. The piece was called "The Daring Young Man on the Flying Trapeze," the story of an impoverished young writer, and it ends like this:

> He placed the shining penny on the table, looking upon it with the delight of a miser. How prettily it smiles, he said. Without reading them he looked at the words, *E Pluribus Unum One Cent United States of America*, and turning the penny over, he saw Lincoln and the words, *In God We Trust Liberty 1923*. How beautiful it is, he said.
>
> He became drowsy and felt a ghastly illness coming over his blood, a feeling of nausea and disintegration. Bewildered, he stood beside his bed, thinking that there *is nothing to do but sleep*. Already he felt himself making great strides through the fluid of the earth, swimming away to the beginning. He fell face down upon the bed, saying, I ought first at least to give the coin to some child. A child could buy any number of things with a penny.
>
> Then swiftly, neatly, with the grace of the young man on the trapeze, he was gone from his body. For an eternal moment he was all things at once: the bird, the fish, the rodent, the reptile, and man. An ocean of print undulated endlessly and darkly before him. The city burned. The herded crowd rioted. The earth circled away, and knowing that he did so, he turned his lost face to the empty sky and became dreamless, unalive, perfect.

Unalive is a haunting word, the right word, and pure Saroyan.

In the last of the Rabbit Angstrom books, *Rabbit at Rest*, John Updike reveals his protagonist's impending death at the very beginning:

Standing amid the tan, excited post-Christmas crowd at the Southwest Florida Regional Airport, Rabbit Angstrom has a funny sudden feeling that what he has come to meet, what's floating in unseen about to land, is not his son Nelson and daughter-in-law Pru and their two children but something more ominous and intimately his: his own death, shaped vaguely like an airplane.

Jack London, who lived from 1876 to 1916, was influenced by Zola's hard-hitting realism (and, in turn, influenced Hemingway). In 1908 London wrote one of the finest action stories ever written, called "To Build a Fire."

The man—he isn't given a name—is making a routine trek in Alaska alone with his dog. The weather turns bad. The man's attempts to build a life-saving fire have all failed, and he finally realizes he may freeze to death:

The sight of the dog put a wild idea into his head. He remembered the tale of the man, caught in a blizzard, who killed a steer and crawled inside the carcass, and so was saved. He would kill the dog and bury his hands in the warm body until the numbness went out of them. Then he could build another fire. He spoke to the dog, calling it to him; but in his voice was a strange note of fear that frightened the animal, who had never known the man to speak in such way before. Something was the matter, and its suspicious nature sensed danger—it knew not what danger, but somewhere, somehow, in its brain arose an apprehension of the man. It flattened its ears down at the sound of the man's voice, and its restless, hunching movements and the liftings and shiftings of its forefeet became more pronounced; but it would not come to the man. He got on his hands and knees and crawled toward the dog. This unusual posture again excited suspicion, and the animal sidled mincingly away.

The man sat up in the snow for a moment and struggled for calmness. Then he pulled on his mittens, by means of his teeth, and got upon his feet. He glanced down at first in order to assure himself that he was really standing up, for the absence of sensation in his feet left him unrelated to the earth. His erect position in itself started to drive the webs of suspicion from the dog's mind; and when he spoke peremptorily, with the sound of whip-lashes in his voice, the dog rendered its customary allegiance and came to him. As it came within reaching distance, the man lost his control. His arms flashed out to the dog, and he experienced genuine surprise when he discovered that his hands could not clutch, that there was neither bend nor feeling in the fingers. He had forgotten for the moment that they were frozen and that they were freezing more and more. All this happened quickly, and before the animal could get away, he encircled its body with his arms. He sat down in the snow, and in this fashion held the dog, while it snarled and whined and struggled.

But it was all he could do, hold its body encircled in his arms and sit there. He realized that he could not kill the dog. There was no way to do it. With his helpless hands he could neither draw nor hold his sheath-knife nor throttle the animal. He released it, and it plunged wildly away, with tail between its legs, and still snarling. It halted forty feet away and surveyed him curiously, with ears sharply pricked forward. The man looked down at his hands in order to locate them, and found them hanging on the ends of his arms. It struck him as curious that one should have to use his eyes in order to find out where his hands were. He began threshing his arms back and forth, beating the mittened hands against his sides. He did this for five minutes, violently, and his heart pumped enough blood up to the surface to put a stop to his shivering. But no sensation was aroused in the hands. He had an impression that they hung like weights on the ends of his arms, but when he tried to run the impression down, he could not find it.

A certain fear of death, dull and oppressive, came to him. This fear quickly became poignant as he realized that it was no longer a mere matter of freezing his fingers and toes, or of losing his hands and feet, but that it was a matter of life and death with the chances against him. This threw him into a panic, and he turned and ran up the creek-bed along the old, dim trail. The dog joined in behind and kept up with him. He ran blindly, without intention, in fear such as he had never known in his life. Slowly, as he ploughed and floundered through the snow, he began to see things again—the banks of the creek, the old timber-jams, the leafless aspens, and the sky. The running made him feel better. He did not shiver. Maybe, if he ran on, his feet would thaw out; and, anyway, if he ran far enough, he would reach camp and the boys. Without doubt he would lose some fingers and toes and some of his face; but the boys would take care of him, and save the rest of him when he got there. And at the same time there was another thought in his mind that said he would never get to the camp and the boys; that it was too many miles away, that the freezing had too great a start on him, and that he would soon be stiff and dead. This thought he kept in the background and refused to consider. Sometimes it pushed itself forward and demanded to be heard, but he thrust it back and strove to think of other things.

It struck him as curious that he could run at all on feet so frozen that he could not feel them when they struck the earth and took the weight of his body. He seemed to himself to skim along above the surface, and to have no connection with the earth. Somewhere he had once seen a winged Mercury, and he wondered if Mercury felt as he felt when skimming over the earth.

His theory of running until he reached camp and the

boys had one flaw in it: he lacked the endurance. Several times he stumbled, and finally he tottered, crumpled up, and fell. When he tried to rise, he failed. He must sit and rest, he decided, and next time he would merely walk and keep on going. As he sat and regained his breath, he noted that he was feeling quite warm and comfortable. He was not shivering, and it even seemed that a warm glow had come to his chest and trunk. And yet, when he touched his nose or cheeks, there was no sensation. Running would not thaw them out. Nor would it thaw out his hands and feet. Then the thought came to him that the frozen portions of his body must be extending. He tried to keep this thought down, to forget it, to think of something else; he was aware of the panicky feeling that it caused, and he was afraid of the panic. But the thought asserted itself, and persisted, until it produced a vision of his body totally frozen. This was too much, and he made another wild run along the trail. Once he slowed down to a walk, but the thought of the freezing extending itself made him run again.

And all the time the dog ran with him, at his heels. When he fell down a second time, it curled its tail over its forefeet and sat in front of him, facing him, curiously eager and intent. The warmth and security of the animal angered him, and he cursed it till it flattened down its ears appeasingly. This time the shivering came more quickly upon the man. He was losing in his battle with the frost. It was creeping into his body from all sides. The thought of it drove him on, but he ran no more than a hundred feet, when he staggered and pitched headlong. It was his last panic. When he had recovered his breath and control, he sat up and entertained in his mind the conception of meeting death with dignity. However, the conception did not come to him in such terms. His idea of it was that he had been making a fool of himself, running around like a chicken with its head cut off—such was the simile that occurred to him. Well, he was bound to freeze anyway, and he might as well take it decently. With this new-found peace of mind came the first glimmerings of drowsiness. A good idea, he thought, to sleep off to death. It was like taking an anæsthetic. Freezing was not so bad as people thought. There were lots worse ways to die.

He pictured the boys finding his body next day. Suddenly he found himself with them, coming along the trail and looking for himself. And, still with them, he came around a turn in the trail and found himself lying in the snow. He did not belong with himself any more, for even then he was out of himself, standing with the boys and looking at himself in the snow. It certainly was cold, was his thought. When he got back to the States he could tell the folks what real cold was. He drifted on from this to a vision of the old-timer on Sulphur Creek. He could see him quite clearly, warm and comfortable, and smoking a pipe.

"You were right, old hoss; you were right," the man mumbled to the old-timer of Sulphur Creek.

Then the man drowsed off into what seemed to him the most comfortable and satisfying sleep he had ever known. The dog sat facing him and waiting. The brief day drew to a close in a long, slow twilight. There were no signs of a fire to be made, and, besides, never in the dog's experience had it known a man to sit like that in the snow and make no fire. As the twilight drew on, its eager yearning for the fire mastered it, and with a great lifting and shifting of forefeet, it whined softly, then flattened its ears down in anticipation of being chidden by the man. But the man remained silent. Later, the dog whined loudly. And still later it crept close to the man and caught the scent of death. This made the animal bristle and back away. A little longer it delayed, howling under the stars that leaped and danced and shone brightly in the cold sky. Then it turned and trotted up the trail in the direction of the camp it knew, where were the other food-providers and fire-providers.

Notice how we see the Freud postulation expressed once more in this unsentimental death:

> He pictured the boys finding his body next day. Suddenly he found himself with them, coming along the trail and looking for himself. . . .

I think the best death scene I've ever read isn't a death scene at all. (I'll explain after you read the following excerpt.)

It comes from a splendid novella written in 1936 by Katherine Anne Porter, called *Pale Horse, Pale Rider*. The story concerns a young journalist, Miranda, who is in love with, and loved by, Adam, a young soldier about to go to war. Toward the end of the story she falls ill with the scourge of World War I, influenza. Adam tries to take care of her, but ultimately she ends up in the hospital where, clearly, she is dying:

> "I know those are your hands," she told Miss Tanner, "I know it, but to me they are white tarantulas, don't touch me."
>
> "Shut your eyes," said Miss Tanner.
>
> "Oh, no," said Miranda, "for then I see worse things," but her eyes closed in spite of her will, and the midnight of her internal torment closed about her.
>
> Oblivion, thought Miranda, her mind feeling among her memories of words she had been taught to describe the unseen, the unknowable, is a whirlpool of gray water turning upon itself for all eternity . . . eternity is perhaps more than the distance to the farthest star. She lay on a narrow ledge over a pit that she knew to be bottomless, though she could

not comprehend it; the ledge was her childhood dream of danger, and she strained back against a reassuring wall of granite at her shoulders, staring into the pit, thinking, There it is, there it is at last, it is very simple; and soft carefully shaped words like oblivion and eternity are curtains hung before nothing at all. I shall not know when it happens, I shall not feel or remember, why can't I consent now, I am lost, there is no hope for me. Look, she told herself, there it is, that is death and there is nothing to fear. But she could not consent, still shrinking stiffly against the granite wall that was her childhood dream of safety, breathing slowly for fear of squandering breath, saying desperately, Look, don't be afraid, it is nothing, it is only eternity.

Granite walls, whirlpools, stars are things. None of them is death, nor the image of it. Death is death, said Miranda, and for the dead it has no attributes. Silenced she sank easily through deeps under deeps of darkness until she lay like a stone at the farthest bottom of life, knowing herself to be blind, deaf, speechless, no longer aware of the members of her own body, entirely withdrawn from all human concerns, yet alive with a peculiar lucidity and coherence; all notions of the mind, the reasonable inquiries of doubt, all ties of blood and the desires of the heart, dissolved and fell away from her, and there remained of her only a minute fiercely burning particle of being that knew itself alone, that relied upon nothing beyond itself for its strength; not susceptible to any appeal or inducement, being itself composed entirely of one single motive, the stubborn will to live. This fiery motionless particle set itself unaided to resist destruction, to survive and to be in its own madness of being, motiveless and planless beyond that one essential end. Trust me, the hard unwinking angry point of light said. Trust me. I stay.

At once it grew, flattened, thinned to a fine radiance, spread like a great fan and curved out into a rainbow through which Miranda, enchanted, altogether believing, looked upon a deep clear landscape of sea and sand, of soft meadow and sky, freshly washed and glistening with transparencies of blue. Why, of course, of course, said Miranda, without surprise but with serene rapture as if some promise made to her had been kept long after she had ceased to hope for it. She rose from her narrow ledge and ran lightly through the tall portals of the great bow that arched in its splendor over the burning blue of the sea and the cool green of the meadow on either hand.

The small waves rolled in and over unhurriedly, lapped upon the sand in silence and retreated; the grasses flurried before a breeze that made no sound. Moving towards her leisurely as clouds through the shimmering air came a great company of human beings, and Miranda saw in an amazement of joy that they were all the living she had known. Their faces were transfigured, each in its own beauty, beyond what she remembered of them, their eyes were clear and untroubled as good weather, and they cast no shadows. They were pure identities and she knew them every one without calling their names or remembering what relation she bore to them. They surrounded her smoothly on silent feet, then turned their entranced faces again towards the sea, and she moved among them easily as a wave among waves. The drifting circle widened, separated, and each figure was alone but not solitary; Miranda, alone too, questioning nothing, desiring nothing, in the quietude of her ecstasy, stayed where she was, eyes fixed on the overwhelming deep sky where it was always morning.

Lying at ease, arms under her head, in the prodigal warmth which flowed evenly from sea and sky and meadow, within touch but not touching the serenely smiling familiar beings about her, Miranda felt without warning a vague tremor of apprehension, some small flick of distrust in her joy; a thin frost touched the edges of this confident tranquillity; something, somebody, was missing, she had lost something, she had left something valuable in another country, oh, what could it be? There are no trees, no trees here, she said in fright, I have left something unfinished. A thought struggled at the back of her mind, came clearly as a voice in her ear. Where are the dead? We have forgotten the dead, oh, the dead, where are they? At once as if a curtain had fallen, the bright landscape faded, she was alone in a strange stony place of bitter cold, picking her way along a steep path of slippery snow, calling out, Oh, I must go back! But in what direction? Pain returned, a terrible compelling pain running through her veins like heavy fire, the stench of corruption filled her nostrils, the sweetish sickening smell of rotting flesh and pus; she opened her eyes and saw pale light through a coarse white cloth over her face, knew that the smell of death was in her own body, and struggled to lift her hand. The cloth was drawn away; she saw Miss Tanner filling a hypodermic needle in her methodical expert way, and heard Dr. Hildesheim saying, "I think that will do the trick. Try another." Miss Tanner plucked firmly at Miranda's arm near the shoulder, and the unbelievable current of agony ran burning through her veins again. She struggled to cry out, saying, Let me go, let me go; but heard only incoherent sounds of animal suffering. She saw doctor and nurse glance at each other with the glance of initiates at a mystery, nodding in silence, their eyes alive with knowledgeable pride. They looked briefly at their handiwork and hurried away.

Bells screamed all off key, wrangling together as they collided in mid air, horns and whistles mingled shrilly with cries of human distress; sulphur colored light exploded through the black window pane and flashed away in darkness. Miranda waking from a dreamless sleep asked without expecting an answer, "What is happening?" for there was a bustle of voices and footsteps in the corridor, and a sharpness in the air; the far clamor went on, a furious exasperated shrieking like a mob in revolt.

The light came on, and Miss Tanner said in a furry voice, "Hear that? They're celebrating. It's the Armistice. The war is over, my dear." Her hands trembled. She rattled a spoon in a cup, stopped to listen, held the cup out to Miranda. From the ward for old bedridden women down the hall floated a ragged chorus of cracked voices singing, "My country, 'tis of thee . . ."

Sweet land . . . oh, terrible land of this bitter world where the sound of rejoicing was a clamor of pain, where ragged tuneless old women, sitting up waiting for their evening bowl of cocoa, were singing, "Sweet land of Liberty—"

"Oh, say, can you see?" their hopeless voices were asking next, the hammer strokes of metal tongues drowning them out. "The war is over," said Miss Tanner, her underlip held firmly, her eyes blurred. Miranda said, "Please open the window, please, I smell death in here."

Don't you feel a little as though you yourself have come back from the dead? *That* is great writing. (Ironically, while Miranda survives, Adam has contracted the influenza from her; before he can go to war, he dies. So the above is not a death scene at all.)

For more excellent action writing, whether featuring death scenes or not, read these novels:

Call of the Wild, Jack London
The Eye of the Needle, Ken Follett
At Play in the Fields of the Lord, Peter Mathiessen
The Big Sleep, Raymond Chandler
Unknown Man Number 89, Elmore Leonard

To Have and Have Not, Ernest Hemingway
Kahawa, Donald Westlake

For detailed death scenes:

Death in Venice, Thomas Mann
Death Comes for the Archbishop, Willa Cather
Death in the Afternoon, Ernest Hemingway
The Dead, James Joyce
Death of a Salesman, Arthur Miller
Most of the short stories of William Faulkner and Ernest
   Hemingway and John Steinbeck.

CHAPTER EIGHT

ENDINGS

As has been avowed, all's well that ends well. In a story well doesn't have to mean *happily*, but all had better end *right*.

But how to end our stories *right*?

We've read the chapter *"Beginnings"*—an essay that advises us to start our stories fast, grab the reader's attention, begin with something happening, hook the reader, and so forth.

Not so easy is the elusive subject of how, when, and where to end a story. Just about the only firm rule one can make is this imprecise admonition:

The endings of stories should satisfy the reader, being consistent with the actions and characterizations that have been shown during the telling of the story.

That is what can be learned from the masters of both short stories and novels.

Consider the disparate endings of some classic stories and you will find they have one thing in common: their ends justify what has gone on before, and usually they stem from the character and actions of the protagonists.

For example, one of the most famous stories ever written

is O. Henry's "Gift of the Magi." It is Christmastime, and a young unselfish couple is very much in love, but also very poor. Each of them wants to surprise the other with a wonderful gift, but how with no money? On Christmas Day they discover that he, in order to buy an ornate comb for her beautiful hair, has sold his cherished pocket watch, while she, to buy a gold chain for his watch, has had her hair cut off and sold it. It is a touching, bittersweet ending which, while sad, is totally right.

There are many conclusions to famous stories and novels that do not "end happily" but which are, nevertheless, satisfying.

Certain stories, even when the protagonist dies a violent death, have "happy" endings because it is appropriate and therefore acceptable to the reader. In Jack London's astonishing story "Lost Face," for example, the hero tricks his captor, the cruel Indian chief, into beheading him, claiming to have a magic potion that will render his neck invulnerable to the chief's axe. The "trick" allows the protagonist to avoid the horribly prolonged torture death the rest of his men have endured:

> Alone, of all their prisoners, he had escaped the torture. That had been the stake for which he played. A great roar of laughter went up. Makamuk bowed his head in shame. The fur-thief had fooled him. He had lost face before all his people. . . . He knew that thenceforth he would be no longer known as Makamuk. He would be Lost Face; the record of his shame would be with him until he died; and whenever the tribes gathered . . . the story would pass back and forth across the camp-fire of how the fur-thief died peaceably, at a single stroke, by the hand of Lost Face.

Because the hero succeeds in outwitting the Indian, he emerges victorious, albeit posthumously, so the ending is entirely satisfactory and not really sad.

Hemingway's novel *For Whom the Bell Tolls* begins this way:

He lay flat on the brown, pine-needled floor of the forest, his chin on his folded arms, and high overhead the wind blew in the tops of the pine trees.

Four hundred seventy pages later, the book ends with Robert Jordan again lying on pine needles, his hip broken, his submachine gun at the ready, awaiting certain death:

Lieutenant Berrendo, watching the trail, came riding up, his thin face serious and grave. His submachine gun lay across his saddle in the crook of his left arm. Robert Jordan lay behind the tree, holding onto himself very carefully and delicately to keep his hands steady. He was waiting until the officer reached the sunlit place where the first trees of the pine forest joined the green slope of the meadow. He could feel his heart beating against the pine needle floor of the forest.

The end.

Once again, it is a sad ending but a correct one. As we would expect him to, Jordan was willing to give his young life for a cause he believed in.

The next two examples point up the vital issue about endings: when and how should the final scene of a story or a novel end. This, of course, depends on the needs of the storyline itself.

In *For Whom the Bell Tolls*, Hemingway felt that the reader did not need to see the actual death of Robert Jordan and its aftermath; it was neither artistic nor necessary to show it. So he didn't. In Hemingway's *A Farewell to Arms*, on the other hand, after the protagonist's beloved Catherine dies in childbirth, in long and detailed scenes, Hemingway even adds a touching conclusion. It is said that he rewrote it some thirty-three times in order to get it right and with the proper restraint. The devastated narrator goes to the hospital room where the dead woman lies and says to the nurses:

"You get out," I said. "The other one too."

But after I had got them out and shut the door and turned off the light it wasn't any good. It was like saying good-by to a statue. After a while I went out and left the hospital and walked back to the hotel in the rain.

How right that simple ending is, especially when we look at some of the other endings which were—mercifully—discarded:

That is all there is to the story [read one reject]. Catherine died and you will die and I will die and that is all I can promise you.

In another, he wallowed in bitterness:

See Naples and die is a fine idea: You will live to hate its guts if you live there. Perhaps there is no luck in a Peninsula.

Sometimes he waxed philosophical:

That is all there is to this story. There is supposed to be something which controls all these things and not one sparrow is forgotten before God.

One ending was verbose in the extreme:

After people die you have to bury them but you do not have to write about it. You do not have to write about an undertaker. Nor the business of burial in a foreign country. Nor do you have to write about that day and the next night nor the day after nor the night after nor all the days after and all the nights after while numbness turns to snow and snow blunts with use. In writing you have a certain choice that you do not have in life.

So, when to end a final scene? What to leave to the reader's imagination? What *feels* right varies from story to story. Some can be ended obliquely, especially when the moral or tangible issues are broad. Other stories—plot-driven stories with specific payoff devices—demand a more "on-the-nose" expository conclusion. A story by Raymond Carver would seem heavy-handed if it didn't end on an oblique note; a Frederick Forsythe short story demands specificity in the payoff.

For example, in a story that ends in a suicide, it is not obligatory that the readers see the act itself. In my novel *Dangerfield*, I planted the fact several times that although the great writer had been sober for many years, if he were to drink again doctors said he would die. At the end of the book, his son finds the locked liquor cabinet smashed open and several bottles gone. That is all the reader needed to know about what was tantamount to a suicide, and I felt it was a more artistic way to end the book because it invited the reader to use his imagination rather than following the man to his last boozy gasp.

On the other hand, Ambrose Bierce in his classic short story "An Occurrence at Owl Creek Bridge" feels obliged to give us every last graphic minute of the young soldier Peyton Farquhar's execution.

In the opening paragraph Farquhar is about to be hanged from the bridge. He thinks of escaping; it then appears that he does break loose and makes his way down the river to his home and to his beloved wife:

At the bottom of the steps she stands waiting, with a smile of ineffable joy, an attitude of matchless grace and dignity. Ah, how beautiful she is! He springs forward with extended arms. As he is about to clasp her he feels a stunning blow upon the back of the neck; a blinding white light blazes all about him with a sound like the shock of a cannon—then all is darkness and silence!

Peyton Farquhar was dead; his body, with a broken neck, swung gently from side to side beneath the timbers of the Owl Creek Bridge.

The reader then realizes that the escape was all in his mind, that there was no escape from death for many of the young men in the Civil War, and that war is hell.

Another famous story is Shirley Jackson's 1948 shocker, "The Lottery." A nice "normal" New England town has an annual lottery after which the owner of the losing ticket is ritually stoned to death; the last chilling sentence is:

"It isn't fair, it isn't right," Mrs. Hutchinson screamed, and then they were upon her.

One of the most famous endings of yesteryear occurred in Noël Coward's play *Cavalcade*. A shocker, it comes after a love scene between Edward Marryot and Edith Harris, his new bride, as they stand in their evening clothes at the rail of an ocean liner:

EDITH: It's too big, the Atlantic, isn't it?
EDWARD: Far too big.
EDITH: And too deep.
EDWARD: Much, much too deep.
EDITH: I don't care a bit, do you?
EDWARD: Not a scrap.
EDITH: Wouldn't it be awful if a magician came to us and

said: "Unless you count accurately every single fish in the Atlantic you die to-night?"

EDWARD: We should die to-night.

As they exit, Edith picks up her cloak from the rail. It has been covering a life belt labelled "S.S. Titanic."

The message to writers here is clear: when your story is intended to frighten or shock the readers, make sure you have a scene in which a character is vulnerable to some imminent danger.

Some oft-anthologized stories depend totally on their surprise endings—tales like Faulkner's "A Rose for Emily," in which an eccentric woman is jilted by her lover and becomes a recluse in her big house. We are given a clue when Miss Emily buys some rat poison early in the story, but we don't have all the information until the end—the *very* end after her funeral:

Already we knew that there was one room in that region above stairs which no one had seen in forty years, and which would have to be forced. They waited until Miss Emily was decently in the ground before they opened it.

The violence of breaking down the door seemed to fill this room with pervading dust. A thin, acrid pall as of the tomb seemed to lie everywhere upon this room decked and furnished as for a bridal: upon the valence curtains of faded rose color, upon the rose-shaded lights, upon the dressing table, upon the delicate array of crystal and the man's toilet things backed with tarnished silver, silver so tarnished that the monogram was obscured. Among them lay a collar and tie, as if they had just been removed, which, lifted, left upon the surface a pale crescent in the dust. Upon a chair hung the suit, carefully folded; beneath it the two mute shoes and the discarded socks.

The man himself lay in the bed.

For a long while we just stood there, looking down at the profound and fleshless grin. The body had apparently once lain in the attitude of an embrace, but now the long sleep that outlasts love, that conquers even the grimace of love, had cuckolded him. What was left of him, rotted beneath what was left of the nightshirt, had become inextricable from the bed in which he lay; and upon him and upon the pillow beside him lay that even coating of the patient and biding dust.

Then we noticed that in the second pillow was the indentation of a head. One of us lifted something from it, and leaning forward, that faint and invisible dust dry and acrid in the nostrils, we saw a long strand of iron-gray hair.

In Roald Dahl's "A Lamb to Slaughter," a matronly murderer gets rid of the murder weapon, a frozen lamb shank, by serving it to the detectives for dinner, which makes for a wry ending and brings a smile. On the other hand, in W. W. Jacobs's classic "The Monkey's Paw," when the third magic wish that the old couple makes to restore their son to them results in his almost returning in his decayed dead state, the ending chills. Most of O. Henry's stories depend upon a twist or surprise at the end.

I confess to a weakness for this kind of a story; I still love a tale with a beginning, middle, and snapper at the end, but over the years stories with the so-called O. Henry endings have fallen into disfavor. There are, however, still magazines around, like *Alfred Hitchcock's Mystery Magazine* and *Ellery Queen's Mystery Magazine*, which specialize in this genre.

Few novels have ending sentences as famous as their opening ones. An exception is Charles Dickens's *Tale of Two Cities*, which begins:

It was the best of times, it was the worst of times. . . .

And the book ends at the guillotine with Sydney Carton's lyr-
ical thoughts (he does not speak them, as many people think):

> "It is a far, far better thing that I do, than I have ever done;
> it is a far, far better rest that I go to than I have ever known."

Some writers, like Mark Twain, like to tie up all loose ends
neatly at the end of their stories. In *Huckleberry Finn*, which
starts out with Huck chatting amiably with the reader, Twain
wraps up matters in a similar folksy way:

> Tom's most well now, and got his bullet around his neck
> on a watch-guard for a watch, and is always seeing what
> time it is, and so there ain't nothing more to write about,
> and I am rotten glad of it, because if I'd 'a' knowed what
> a trouble it was to make a book I wouldn't 'a' tackled it,
> and ain't a-going to no more. But I reckon I got to light out
> for the Territory ahead of the rest, because Aunt Sally she's
> going to adopt me and sivilize me, and I can't stand it. I
> been there before.

W. H. Auden said that no two people ever read the same
book; in a similar way, perhaps, no two people would ever
agree on where or how a story should end. For example,
Hemingway loved *Huckleberry Finn*, saying:

> All American writing comes from that. There was noth-
> ing before. There has been nothing as good since.

Yet he hated the ending:

> If you read it you must stop where the Nigger Jim is sto-
> len from the boys. That is the real end. The rest is just
> cheating.

At least one story, which is over a century old, leaves the ending entirely up to the reader: Frank Stockton's "The Lady or the Tiger?" tells of a jealous princess who must choose whether a beautiful young bride for her lover will come out of a tunnel in the arena—or a vicious tiger that will claw him to bits; the story has prompted many a heated debate over why her choice would be for the one or the other. It is one of the most famous stories ever written. Get it from the library today!

Though perhaps not classics, we remember many of the endings of plays and films such as *Casablanca*:

> "Louis, I have the feeling this is the beginning of a beautiful friendship."

Or when the Wizard of Oz is exposed as a fraud:

> "I'm not a bad man, my dear, just a bad wizard."

Or Joe E. Brown's response in *Some Like It Hot*, when he is told the object of his passion is a man in drag:

> "Nobody's perfect!"

Or the second act closer of *The Front Page*:

> "That son of a bitch stole my watch!"

Or the bittersweet and tender ending of Robert Anderson's play (and film) *Tea and Sympathy* when the boarding school teacher's wife gives herself to the schoolboy who'd been humiliated to restore his belief in himself and his manhood:

> LAURA *seeing a bolt on the door, slides it to. Then she stands looking at* TOM, *her hand at her neck. With a slight*

and delicate movement, she unbuttons the top button of her blouse, and moves toward TOM. *When she gets alongside the bed, she reaches out her hand, still keeping one hand at her blouse.* TOM *makes no move. Just watches her.*

LAURA *makes a little move with the outstretched hand, asking for his hand.* TOM *slowly moves his hand to hers.*

LAURA *(Stands there holding his hand and smiling gently at him. Then she sits and looks down at the boy, and after a moment, barely audible)*:
And now ... nothing?

TOM*'s other hand comes up and with both his hands he brings her hand to his lips.*

LAURA *(Smiles tenderly at this gesture, and after a moment)*: Years from now ... when you talk about this ... and you will ... be kind.

Gently she brings the boy's hands toward her opened blouse, as the lights slowly dim out ... and ...

THE CURTAIN FALLS

One wrong action, one word too many, and the scene would have caused laughter. As it was, it was a superb exercise in taste and restraint.

Emile Zola, the great French journalist who lived from 1840 to 1902, is best known for his crucial role in the notorious Dreyfus case. But his novel *Nana*, about a prostitute, was a bombshell of a book in its time. He also wrote many short stories of action and death in a naturalistic style that influenced the direction and style of modern writing.

In his war story "The Attack on the Mill," the Prussians have taken over an old mill because a young sniper, Dominique, has killed several of their soldiers from that vantage point. They have taken him prisoner as well as his fiancée, Françoise, and her father the miller, called Father Merlier, and have threatened to shoot them all.

Here is how it ends, and notice how the narrative has been constructed so as to finish with a single repeated word:

It was three o'clock. The heavens were piled high with great black clouds, the tail-end of a storm that had been raging somewhere in the vicinity. Beneath the coppery sky and ragged scud the valley of Rocreuse, so bright and smiling in the sunlight, became a grim chasm, full of sinister shadows. The Prussian officer had done nothing with Dominique beyond placing him in confinement, giving no indication of his ultimate purpose in regard to him. Françoise, since noon, had been suffering unendurable agony; notwithstanding her father's entreaties, she would not leave the courtyard. She was waiting for the French troops to appear, but the hours slipped by, night was approaching, and she suffered all the more since it appeared as if the time thus gained would have no effect on the final result.

About three o'clock, however, the Prussians began to make their preparations for departure. The officer had gone to Dominique's room and remained closeted with him for some minutes, as he had done the day before. Françoise knew that the young man's life was hanging in the balance; she clasped her hands and put up fervent prayers. Beside her sat Father Merlier, rigid and silent, declining, like the true peasant he was, to attempt any interference with accomplished facts.

"Oh! my God! my God!" Françoise exclaimed, "they are going to kill him!"

The miller drew her to him, and took her on his lap as if she had been a little child. At this juncture the officer came from the room, followed by two men conducting Dominique between them.

"Never, never!" the latter exclaimed. "I am ready to die."

"You had better think the matter over," the officer replied. "I shall have no trouble in finding someone else to render us the service which you refuse. I am generous with you; I offer you your life. It is simply a matter of guiding us across the forest to Montredon; there must be paths."

Dominique made no answer.

"Then you persist in your obstinacy?"

"Shoot me, and let's have done with it," he replied.

Françoise, in the distance, entreated her lover with clasped hands; she was forgetful of all considerations save one—she would have had him commit a treason. But Father Merlier seized her hands, that the Prussians might not see the wild gestures of a woman whose mind was disordered by her distress.

"He is right," he murmured, "it is best for him to die."

The firing party was in readiness. The officer still had hopes of bringing Dominique over, and was waiting to see him exhibit some signs of weakness. Deep silence prevailed. Heavy peals of thunder were heard in the distance, the fields and woods lay lifeless beneath the sweltering heat. And it was in the midst of this oppressive silence that suddenly the cry arose: "The French! The French!"

It was a fact; they were coming. The line of red trousers could be seen advancing along the Sauval road, at the edge of the forest. In the mill the confusion was extreme; the Prussian soldiers ran to and fro, giving vent to guttural cries. Not a shot had been fired as yet.

"The French! The French!" cried Françoise, clapping her hands for joy. She was like a woman possessed. She had escaped from her father's embrace and was laughing boisterously, her arms raised high in the air. They had come at last, then, and had come in time, since Dominique was still there, alive!

A crash of musketry that rang in her ears like a thunderclap caused her to suddenly turn her head. The officer had muttered, "We will finish this business first," and with his own hands pushing Dominique up against the wall of a shed, had given the command to the squad to fire. When Françoise turned, Dominique was lying on the ground, pierced by a dozen bullets.

She did not shed a tear; she stood there like one suddenly rendered senseless. Her eyes were fixed and staring, and she went and seated herself beneath the shed, a few steps from the lifeless body. She looked at it wistfully; now and then she would make a movement with her hands in an aimless, childish way. The Prussians had seized Father Merlier as a hostage.

It was a pretty fight. The officer, perceiving that he could not retreat without being cut to pieces, rapidly made the best disposition possible of his men; it was as well to sell their lives dearly. The Prussians were now the defenders of the mill, and the French were the attacking party. The musketry fire began with unparalleled fury; for half an hour there was no lull in the storm. Then a deep report was heard, and a ball carried away a main branch of the old elm. The French had artillery; a battery, in position just beyond the ditch where Dominique had concealed himself, commanded the main street of Rocreuse. The conflict could not last long after that.

Ah! the poor old mill! The cannon balls raked it from wall to wall. Half the roof was carried away; two of the walls fell in. But it was on the side towards the Morelle that the damage was most lamentable. The ivy, torn from the tottering walls, hung in tatters, débris of every description floated away upon the bosom of the stream, and through a great breach Françoise's chamber was visible, with its little bed, the snow-white curtains of which were carefully drawn. Two balls struck the old wheel in quick succession, and it gave one parting groan; the buckets were carried away down stream, the frame was crushed into a shapeless mass. It was the soul of the stout old mill parting from the body.

Then the French came forward to carry the place by storm. There was a mad hand-to-hand conflict with the bayonet. Under the dull sky the pretty valley became a huge slaughter-pen; the broad meadows looked on in horror, with their great isolated trees and their rows of poplars, dotting them with shade, while to right and left the forest was like the walls of a tilting ground enclosing the combatants, and in Nature's universal panic the gentle murmur of the springs and watercourses sounded like sobs and wails.

Françoise had not stirred from the shed where she remained hanging over Dominique's body. Father Merlier had met his death from a stray bullet. Then the French captain, the Prussians being exterminated and the mill on fire, entered the courtyard at the head of his men. It was the first success that he had gained since the breaking out of the war, so, all inflamed with enthusiasm, drawing himself up to the full height of his lofty stature, he laughed pleasantly, as a handsome cavalier like him might laugh. Then, perceiving poor idiotic Françoise where she crouched between the corpses of her father and her betrothed, among the smoking ruins of the mill, he saluted her gallantly with his sword, and shouted:

"Victory! Victory!"

Change is an important element in a successful story's ending—things and people and the situation we saw at the beginning are now different. A good example—a chilling example—is Flannery O'Connor's story "A Good Man is Hard to Find," in which readers see a querulous, selfish old woman die a surprisingly brave death at the hands of some criminals:

"She would have been a good woman," The Misfit said, "If it had been somebody there to shoot her every minute of her life."

Sometimes a writer, after tying up the strands of the plot, will add a sort of coda or general summing up of the story. Chekhov once said:

> *My instinct tells me that at the end of a story or a novel I must artfully concentrate for the reader an impression of the entire work.*

Fitzgerald does this in *The Great Gatsby*. After the enigmatic protagonist is dead and buried and the plot has run its course, the narrator ruminates on the tragedy at length, ending with:

> Gatsby believed in the green light, the orgiastic future that year by year recedes before us. It eluded us then, but that's no matter—tomorrow we will run faster, stretch out our arms farther. . . . And one fine morning—
> So we beat on, boats against the current, borne back ceaselessly into the past.

Many stories indicate and almost *require* that at the end the protagonist be killed—shot, like Gatsby, or guillotined, like Sydney Carton, or that virtually everyone die by cold steel as in *Hamlet*; any other ending in those cases would not be satisfactory to the reader bearing in mind what has gone on before.

So many of the great stories end, as with real life, in a death scene, whether from natural causes, murder, suicide, war, at the hands of nature, or an animal.

Perhaps the most realistic suicide scene ever written is

Emma Bovary's. Flaubert chronicles every harrowing moment of his heroine's demise after she takes the arsenic:

> "Ah, it's nothing very much—dying!" she thought. "I shall just drop off to sleep, and it will all be over."

But not at all. Flaubert knew a great deal about medicine, having observed his doctor father at his trade, and in the final pages of *Madame Bovary* he spares the reader nothing:

> She kept her senses alert, wondering whether she had any pain. But no! Nothing yet. She could hear the clock ticking, the fire flickering. Charles was standing by the bed, and she heard the sound of his breathing.
>
> "Ah, it's nothing very much—dying!" she thought. "I shall just drop off to sleep, and it will all be over."
>
> She gulped down a draught of water and turned her face to the wall.
>
> But there was still that horrible taste of ink.
>
> "I'm thirsty ... oh, I'm so dreadfully thirsty!" she sighed.
>
> "What can it be?" said Charles, bringing her a glass of water.
>
> "It's nothing.... Open the window.... I can't breathe."
>
> And she began to vomit so suddenly that she hardly had time to snatch her handkerchief from under her pillow.
>
> "Take it away!" she said quickly. "Throw it somewhere."
>
> He questioned her. She made no answer. She kept perfectly still, for fear the slightest movement should cause her to be sick. And she was beginning to feel an icy coldness, creeping up from her feet to her heart.
>
> "Ah, it's beginning now!" she whispered.
>
> "What's that you say?"
>
> She kept swaying her head, gently, from side to side, in

a state of anguish, continually opening and shutting her jaws, as if she had something very heavy on her tongue. At eight o'clock the vomiting began again.

Charles, examining the basin, noticed a sort of whitish slime that clung to the bottom.

"That's extraordinary, that's very odd!" he observed.

"No, no, you're wrong," she said in a strong voice.

Then very lightly, almost as if he were caressing her, he passed his hand over her stomach. She gave a piercing shriek. He started back, scared out of his wits.

Then she began to moan, weakly at first. Her shoulders were shuddering convulsively, and she was growing paler than the sheet she was grasping with her clenched hands. Her pulse was irregular and, by this time, almost imperceptible.

There were drops of sweat on her livid face, that seemed as though it were petrified in the exhalation of some metallic vapour. Her teeth were chattering, her eyes were dilated and staring vaguely about her, and every question she answered with a shake of the head. She even smiled two or three times. Gradually her groans grew louder. Once she tried to stifle a shriek; she pretended she was getting better and would be getting up. But she was taken with convulsions again.

"Oh, God, it's frightful!"

He flung himself on his knees at her bedside.

"Tell me, what have you been eating? For God's sake, speak!" and as he looked at her there was a tenderness in his eyes she had never seen in them before.

For many pages we go on agonizing horribly with Emma, only occasionally cutting away to the people around her, especially to her naive, devoted, long-suffering husband, Charles:

"Perhaps, after all, we ought not to despair," thought he.

And indeed she looked all round about her, slowly, like one waking from a dream; then, in quite a strong voice, she asked for her mirror, and remained looking into it for some time, until great tears began to trickle from her eyes. Then she sighed, turned away her head, and sank down again on the pillow.

And immediately her breathing became very rapid. The full length of her tongue protruded from her mouth. Her wandering eyes began to grow pale, like a pair of lamp globes in which the light was waning, so that you would have thought her already dead, but for the terrible heaving of her sides, shaken by some raging tempest, as though the soul were leaping and straining to be free. Félicité knelt down before the crucifix, and even the apothecary bent his hams a little, while Monsieur Canivet stood gazing out vaguely on to the Square. Bournisien had begun to pray again, his face bowed down upon the edge of the bed, his long black soutane trailing out behind him across the floor. Charles was on the other side, on his knees, his arms outstretched towards Emma. He had taken her hands, and was pressing them in his, trembling at her every heart-beat, as a man might start at the sound of a collapsing ruin. As the death-rattle grew more insistent, the priest redoubled the speed of his orisons; they mingled with Bovary's choking sobs, and sometimes all seemed drowned in the low murmur of the Latin syllables, which sounded like the tinkling of a passing bell.

Suddenly there was a noise of heavy clogs on the pavement outside and the scraping of a stick, and a voice, a raucous voice, began to sing,

Now skies are bright, the summer's here,
A maiden thinks upon her dear.

Emma sat bolt upright like a corpse suddenly galvanized into life, her hair dishevelled, her eyes fixed in a glassy stare, gaping with horror.

And to gather up with care
What the weary reaper leaves,
My Nanette goes gleaning there,
Down among the golden sheaves.

"The blind man!" she cried, and broke out into a laugh—a ghastly, frantic, despairing laugh—thinking she saw the hideous features of the wretched being, rising up to strike terror to her soul, on the very threshold of eternal night.

She stooped low, the wind blew high,
What a sight for mortal eye!

She fell back in a paroxysm on to the mattress. They hurried to her side. Emma was no more.

This is not the end of the novel, as you might expect, for even after Emma is no more, Flaubert takes no pity on us and gives us several painful pages of funeral and "the why" aftermath, and none of it is boring in the hands of this great writer. If you don't read another classic, read *Madame Bovary*.

E. M. Forster, in his *Aspects of the Novel*, has written:

The treatment of death . . . is nourished much more on observation, and has a variety about it which suggests that the novelist finds it congenial. He does, for the reason that death ends a book neatly, and for the less obvious reason that working as he does in time he finds it easier to work from the known towards the darkness rather than from the darkness of birth towards the known. By the time his characters die, he understands them, he can be both appropriate and imaginative about them—strongest of combinations. Take a little death—the death of Mrs. Proudie in the *Last Chronicle of Barset*. All is in keeping, yet the effect is terrifying, because Trollope has ambled Mrs. Proudie down many a diocesan bypath, showing her paces, making her snap, accustoming us, even to boredom, to her character and tricks, to her "Bishop, consider the souls of the people," and then she has a heart attack by the edge of her bed, she has ambled far enough,—end of Mrs. Proudie. There is scarcely anything that the novelist cannot borrow from "daily death"; scarcely anything he may not profitably invent.

But, of course, things don't *always* have to end badly in fiction. There are many happy endings in great literature. Alice returns safe and sound from Wonderland, "and she would remember the happy summer days." We know Scarlett O'Hara is going to make it somehow, with or without Rhett Butler; Don Quixote gets back to La Mancha in one piece; Ulysses makes it home and slays his wife's suitors; Tom Jones ends up with the girl and the money; and Elizabeth nabs Darcy in *Pride and Prejudice*.

Evelyn Waugh was noted for his delightful and sometimes bizarre endings, such as in the novella *The Loved One*, where the human corpse gets mixed up with a pet cemetery; *Black Mischief*, where the hero ends up unwittingly eating his fiancée served up by cannibals; and his masterpiece, *A Handful of Dust*, where the protagonist somehow finds himself enslaved to a madman in the Brazilian jungle and daily reading to him all of Dickens over and over for the rest of his life.

Endings like Waugh's, or like Saki's or O. Henry's, defy

categorization and only prove how futile it is to try to recommend any method of ending a story.

Most good stories end the way they *must* end; the agendas of the protagonists or antagonists dictate the outcome, and in this way the endings satisfy the reader. Many beginning writers, instead of having the characters decide the outcome, bring in Mother Nature (or the Marines) to help them wind up things tidily: a well-timed earthquake, or a flood, storm, or forest fire. The gods stepping in, *deus ex machina*, rarely satisfies, except, perhaps, on the wide, wide silver screen.

Totally unsatisfactory is the ending, no matter for what age the story is written, "And then he (or she) woke up, for it had all been just a dream."

Also, using a coincidence to resolve matters rarely satisfies; you may *launch* a story with a coincidence ("Honey, you're not going to believe this, but two seats ahead of us in this very plane to Paris sits my first wife!") but do not *conclude* a story or solve your plot with a coincidence.

Here are some other caveats:

Don't moralize.

Don't intrude your omniscient judgment of your characters' behavior; you are supposed to be neutral, a referee. Remember Tolstoy's observation: "I have found that my most successful stories have been those where the reader did not know whose side I was on."

Don't have your protagonist act out of character.

For example, Dickens subtly prepared us well for Sydney Carton's "sudden" redemption in *A Tale of Two Cities* and his "It is a far, far better thing that I do. . . ."

Don't feel you must tie up all the loose ends.

For example: "David Copperfield went on to win the Booker Prize, Agnes became a suffragette, Uriah Heep found God," and so forth. The reader should have enough clues to envision the future of the principals once the book is closed or "The End" appears after the climax of a short story.

Don't go on too long.

The temptation to dawdle and not release the children of one's imagination should be resisted. Do not cut off the dog's tail an inch at a time. Suppose, for example, Hemingway had not concluded *The Sun Also Rises* with that lovely and appropriate death knell of a line, "Isn't it pretty to think so," but instead, anticlimactically, had caused Jake and Lady Brett to go to a hotel and *prove* that their marriage would never have worked.

As Shakespeare advised: "Do not stand upon the order of your going, but go at once."

Don't explain too much.

Most readers are alert to clues along the way and enjoy a story more if they are not clubbed over the head by long explanations. A good example, speaking literally of clubbing, is Roald Dahl's short story "Lamb to the Slaughter," mentioned earlier in this chapter: Mary Maloney has killed her abusive husband with a frozen leg of lamb and then serves it to the policemen who are searching her house for the murder weapon. One of them belches as they eat the evidence with gusto and says:

"Personally, I think it's right here on the premises."
"Probably right under our very noses. What you think, Jack?"
And in the other room, Mary Maloney began to giggle.

The end.

We do not need to stay for dessert at this particular meal; the story is over, we chuckle, and are more than satisfied.

And that is the operative word. Whether the hero or heroine lives or, like Romeo and Juliet, dies, whether the villain does or does not achieve his objectives, whether happy or sad, the end of the story must *satisfy*.

And always keep in mind Longfellow's words:

Great is the art of the beginning, but greater the art of ending.

CHAPTER NINE

TITLES

"Aside from making your literary product unique and serving as sort of a trademark," Sinclair Lewis once told me, "the primary function of a title is to lure unsuspecting readers into having a go at your story."

In spite of titling being the most imprecise, capricious, and subjective component of a story, most people have definite ideas of what a good title is or should be.

In hindsight, and after millions of copies have been sold, it is easy to say, for example, that *The Catcher in the Rye* is a great title.

But supposing you were the first person to hear J. D. Salinger propose that, as the handle for his first novel, he wanted that peculiar juxtaposition of words—especially since there is no catcher and no rye in the story (except as a misunderstanding of the words of the old Scottish ditty "Comin' Through the Rye").

Would you rush out to buy a book called *Pansy*? That is what *Gone with the Wind* was called up until six months of publication by the Macmillan Company. At the last moment Margaret Mitchell changed it to *Tote the Weary Load*. Other titles followed in rapid succession: *Milestones*; *Ba! Ba! Black Sheep*; and *Jettison*. It has been said that eighteen titles in all were considered before the author found *Gone with the Wind* in Ernest Dowson's poem "Cynara."

Would we think the trite phrase "gone with the wind" so memorable if the novel had sold, say, only hundreds of books instead of multi-millions?

As Somerset Maugham said so accurately:

A good title is the title of a book that's successful.

Maugham's title of one of his many successful novels, based loosely on Paul Gauguin, was *The Moon and Sixpence*:

People tell me it's a good title but they don't know what it means. It means reaching for the moon and missing the sixpence at one's feet.

It is not always necessary that a title be understood for it to be a good title.

Writers may not always be the best judges of the appropriate title for their work. Maugham had originally titled his masterpiece not *Of Human Bondage* but *Beauty and Ashes*, then ultimately discovered it had already been taken. F. Scott Fitzgerald wanted to call his 1924 masterpiece about the jazz age, first, *Hurrah for the Red, White and Blue*, and then, *Trimalchio in West Egg*. (In Petronius's *Satyricon*, Trimalchio was a rich and sybaritic patron.) The great editor Maxwell Perkins didn't like the titles, and Fitzgerald offered others: *The High-Bouncing Lover* and *The Gold-Hatted Gatsby*. These were inspired by the little poem by "Thomas Parke D'Invilliers" (Fitzgerald himself) that he quoted on the title page:

Then wear the gold hat, if that will move her;
If you can bounce high, bounce for her too,

Till she cry, "Lover, gold-hatted, high-bouncing lover,
I must have you!"

Cooler heads prevailed, and the novel came out as *The Great Gatsby* to resounding and permanent acclaim. But even after publication Fitzgerald protested that *Trimalchio in West Egg* was a better title.

Walker Percy said that a good title "should be like a good metaphor; it should intrigue without being too baffling or too obvious."

Some titles *are* baffling until we have read the book—and sometimes even afterward: *A Clockwork Orange, Catch-22, Kaputt, Shibumi, The Milagro Beanfield War, Like Water for Chocolate, The Unbearable Lightness of Being, Smilla's Sense of Snow*, and so on.

Their very unfamiliarity and strangeness is calculated to lure us into finding out what the story is about.

Sometimes the esoteric titles with bizarre combinations of words backfire, and customers shy away from them. Overly cute juxtapositions—such as *The Passionate Frigidaire, With Wings Astern*, and *The Reluctant Iguana*—might turn off more readers than they intrigue.

Just where do titles come from—and when?

Sinclair Lewis told me: "Give your story a title right away, sort of a handle to carry it around in your mind with. You'll change it eventually."

I was writing my first novel and calling it *Christmas in July*. When that title was found to be taken, I asked Mr. Lewis for help.

"Well, your hero and his girl live in a house called La Villa Inocenta," he said. "How about calling the book *The Innocent Villa*?"

The title didn't make much sense, but it suggested an exotic locale and was intriguingly different. The publisher,

Random House, went with it, and the book had a fairly successful run for a first novel.

Sinclair Lewis himself had originally entitled *Main Street*, which has passed into everyone's lexicon, *The Village Virus*.

Would that book have made the same impact under the first title? One cannot know. Similarly, another Lewis title, *Babbitt*, has also gone into dictionaries as: "A business or professional man who conforms unthinkingly to prevailing middle-class standards" *(Merriam-Webster's Collegiate Dictionary)*.

But would Lewis's original title have made Webster's? It was: *Pumphrey*.

"The title comes last," said Tennessee Williams.

Hemingway said: "I make a list of titles *after* I've finished the story or book—sometimes as many as a hundred. Then I start eliminating them, sometimes all of them."

One is frequently amazed at the terrible first choices of famous novelists for their offspring. Charles Dickens's classic novel that ended up as *Bleak House* he originally wanted to call *Tom-All-Alone's The Ruined House*; and his *Hard Times* started out as *Two and Two Are Four*.

Where does the imagination for a great title come from?

Many writers find their title in the body of the work itself, perhaps in the dialogue. One of the titles Margaret Mitchell had thought of for *Gone with the Wind* was *Tomorrow Is Another Day*, a cliché taken from Scarlett's thoughts.

Many titles have come from nursery rhymes such as *When the Bough Breaks*, *The Cradle Will Fall*, and so forth. Ed McBain has written a dozen crime books with titles like *Puss in Boots*, *Cinderella*, *Mary, Mary*, and *Jack and the Beanstalk*.

Over the years, Shakespeare has been one of the most tapped, and seemingly inexhaustible, sources of titles: *Something Wicked This Way Comes*, *Cakes and Ale*, *Remembrance of Things Past, The Sound and the Fury, The Dogs of War, The Winter of Our Discontent, To Thine Own Self Be True.*

Great poets, such as Keats, Byron, Pope, Gray, Frost, and Walt Whitman have been rich sources for titles. Thomas Wolfe's title *Look Homeward, Angel* came from a line in Milton's "Lycidas," but only after such titles as *They Are Strange, They Are Lost* and *The Exile's Story* were rejected by his editor, Maxwell Perkins. (Wolfe's wonderful title *You Can't Go Home Again* came not from a poem but a chance remark by a friend.)

Lines from songs have provided good titles: *Blue Skies, From Here to Eternity, Body and Soul.*

The Bible, of course, has been a gold mine, especially Ecclesiastes *(The Sun Also Rises)* and The Song of Solomon *(The Sound of the Turtle).*

Common phrases can make good titles: *I Can Get It for You Wholesale, They Shoot Horses, Don't They, You Could Look It Up, Born Yesterday, Fun While It Lasted.*

Simply using the hero's or heroine's name as a title was more common in the past than today: *Pamela, Tom Jones, Emma, Madame Bovary, Jane Eyre, David Copperfield, Nana, Tom Sawyer, Ivanhoe, Ethan Frome, Jude the Obscure, Anna Karenina.*

But it hasn't gone totally out of fashion in more modern times, witness: *Rebecca, Laura, Lolita, Mrs. Bridge, Elmer Gantry, Youngblood Hawke, Forrest Gump.*

More in fashion are variations using a name, such as: *The Prime of Miss Jean Brodie, The Great Gatsby, Sophie's Choice, Henderson the Rain King, Portnoy's Complaint, What Makes Sammy Run?*

Place names are frequently used in titles, either alone—*USA, Middlemarch, Wuthering Heights, Hawaii, Winesburg, Ohio*—or with other words: *Babylon Revisited, Manhattan Transfer, Barchester Towers, Brideshead Revisited, The Cruel Sea, The Big Sky, The Secret Garden.*

Appomatox would be an adequate title; Bruce Catton's *A Stillness at Appomatox* is a great one.

And I submit that Thornton Wilder's *The Bridge of San Luis Rey* is a far more intriguing title than Robert Waller's *The Bridges of Madison County*. The former is a *specific* bridge (what happened there?!) in an exotic setting; the latter is a generalization of bridges in a rural, not very exciting, area. However, the less than compelling title did not, as we witnessed, hurt the latter's sales.

Some titles instantly bespeak another era; for example, many of Anthony Trollope's: *Can You Forgive Her?*, *He Knew He Was Right, Framley Parsonage*. (On the other hand, though the titles seem old-fashioned, the prose inside those volumes seems far more modern than the times depicted therein. If you've not read Trollope, start with *The Way We Live Now*, a very influential novel.)

Unorthodox titles have been around for a long time, such as John Ford's 1627 tragedy *'Tis Pity She's a Whore* and Samuel Butler's 1872 utopian novel *Erewhon* (an anagram for *Nowhere*). Dylan Thomas's 1954 play about Wales, *Under Milk Wood*, was originally titled *Llareggub*, a Welsh-appearing word, until one reads it backwards.

In recent decades America has seen a spate of bizarre titles: Arthur Kopit's *Oh Dad, Poor Dad, Mama's Hung You in the Closet and I'm Feelin' So Sad* and Richard Fariña's *Been Down So Long It Looks Like Up to Me*. *Who's Afraid of Virginia Woolf?* in 1962 spawned many other bizarre titles. Perhaps influenced by that Edward Albee title, a Broadway play based on my novel *Dangerfield* had its title changed abruptly before the opening by the producer Roger Stevens to *A Bicycle Ride to Nevada*, even though there was no bicycle and no Nevada and no ride in the script. The play lasted an entire night on the Great White Way and then expired, which may or may not have been hastened by its new title.

So when all is said and done, we see that the art of titling is a curious and mercurial and mysterious one.

"Don't worry about your titles," Sinclair Lewis told me. "The publisher will change it anyway. If he doesn't, his wife will."

In the same vein, Raymond Chandler in a letter to Alfred Knopf remarked: "I am trying to think up a good title for you to want me to change."

Personally, I am inclined to agree with James Thurber, who said, referring to a famous story by Irwin Shaw: "All pieces should be called by the best of *New Yorker* titles, 'The Girls in Their Summer Dresses.'"

To show the disparity between some original titles and the one ultimately published, here is a list of well-known works:

Earlier Titles	Published Titles
With Due Respect	*A Moveable Feast*
The Sentimental Education of Frederick Henry	*A Farewell to Arms*
Catch-18	*Catch-22*
Twilight	*The Sound and the Fury*
Blanche's Chair in the Moon	*A Streetcar Named Desire*
Finnerty's Ball	*The Man with the Golden Arm*
They Don't Build Statues to Businessmen	*Valley of the Dolls*
Tenderness	*Lady Chatterley's Lover*
All's Well That Ends Well	*War and Peace*
Four and a Half Years of Struggle Against Lies, Stupidity, and Cowardice	*Mein Kampf*

Earlier Titles	Published Titles
The Last Man in Europe	*1984*
The Mute	*The Heart Is a Lonely Hunter*
Before This Anger	*Roots*
The Birds and the Bees	*Everything You Always Wanted to Know About Sex But Were Afraid to Ask*
The Kingdom by the Sea	*Lolita*
No Safe Harbor	*Ship of Fools*
To Climb the Wall	*The Blackboard Jungle*
The Whale	*Moby-Dick*
Too Late, Beloved!	*Tess of the D'Urbervilles*
Private Fleming, His Various Battles	*The Red Badge of Courage*
Something That Happened	*Of Mice and Men*
The Sea-Cook	*Treasure Island*
The Man That Was a Thing	*Uncle Tom's Cabin*
Bar-B-Que	*The Postman Always Rings Twice*
A Day of Fear	*Matador*

Lastly, consider this: For his new magazine, Charles Dickens planned to write an exciting serial. He immediately encountered title trouble. When he had first conceived the idea for the story he had set down *Time!*, *The Leaves of the Forest*, *Scattered Leaves*, *The Great Wheel*, *Round and Round*, *Old Leaves*, *Long Ago*, *Far Apart*, *Fallen Leaves*, *Five and Twenty*

*Years, Years and Years, Day After Day, Felled Trees, Memory
Carton, Rolling Stones, Two Generations.*
Later he considered other possibilities: *One of These Days,
Buried Alive, The Thread of Gold, The Doctor of Beauvais.*
And then, on March 11, 1859, he wrote a friend:

I have got exactly the name for the story that is wanted;
exactly what will fit the opening to a T:
A Tale of Two Cities.

SUGGESTIONS FOR FURTHER READING

Any list of "must-read" stories for writers is, of course, purely subjective. But I believe that most professional writers would agree that this smorgasbord of short stories is a sound one. Herewith, alphabetically and with asterisks on my favorites, is my list:

"A and P," John Updike
"Act of Faith," "Girls in Their Summer Dresses," Irwin Shaw
"The Basement Room," Graham Greene
"Big Blonde," "The Cost of Living," Dorothy Parker
"Blind Love," V. S. Pritchett
*"The Catbird Seat," James Thurber
"Champion," Ring Lardner
*"A Face in the Crowd," Budd Schulberg
*"The Five-Forty-Eight," John Cheever
"The Gift of the Magi," "The Ransom of Red Chief," O. Henry
"The Gold Bug," "The Tell-Tale Heart," Edgar Allan Poe
"A Good Man Is Hard to Find," Flannery O'Connor

*"Handcarved Coffins," Truman Capote
*"The Illustrated Man," "The Lake," Ray Bradbury
 "Johnny Bear," "The Red Pony," John Steinbeck
 "The Lady or the Tiger," Frank Stockton
*"The Lady with the Toy Dog," Anton Chekhov
 "Lamb to the Slaughter," Roald Dahl
 "The Legacy," "The Necklace," Guy de Maupassant
 "The Lottery," Shirley Jackson
 "The Man Who Would Be King," Rudyard Kipling
 "Maria Concepción," "Noon Wine," Katherine Anne Porter
 "Metamorphosis," Franz Kafka
 "The Monkey's Paw," W. W. Jacobs
 "Mr. Morgan," James Michener
 "An Occurrence at Owl Creek Bridge," Ambrose Bierce
 "Odour of Chrysanthemums," D. H. Lawrence
 "The Open Boat," Stephen Crane
 "The Open Window," "Tobermory," Saki
 "Powerhouse," "Why I Live at the P.O.," Eudora Welty
 "Rain," "Red," Somerset Maugham
*"The Rich Boy," "Bernice Bobs Her Hair," F. Scott Fitz-
   gerald
 "A Rose for Emily," "The Bear," William Faulkner
*"The Short Happy Life of Francis Macomber," "The Un-
   defeated," Ernest Hemingway
 "Silent Snow, Secret Snow," Conrad Aiken
*"To Build a Fire," Jack London
 "Uncle Wiggily in Connecticut," J. D. Salinger
 "Wet Saturday," John Collier

If I have left out any of your favorite stories or your favorite writers, forgive me.

In a more contemporary vein, here are a few suggestions:

"A Vintage Thunderbird," Ann Beattie
"At the Jack Randa Hotel," Alice Munro

"Bluebeard's Egg," Margaret Atwood
"The Emperor of the Air," Ethan Canin
"Engagements," Tama Janowitz
*"The Famous Toboggan of Laughter," Ella Leffland
"Happy Families Are All Alike," Peter Taylor
"Him with His Foot in His Mouth," Saul Bellow
*"How to Skin a Cat," Thomas McGuane
"Idaho," Barry Hannah
*"Legends of the Fall," Jim Harrison
"The Liar," Tobias Wolff
"Lovers of Their Time," William Trevor
*"No Comebacks," Frederic Forsyth
"The Pugilist at Rest," Thom Jones
"The Rake People," Judith Freeman
"Red Fish," Rick Bass
"Shiloh," Bobbie Ann Mason
"Superior Women," Alice Adams
"Victory Over Japan," Ellen Gillchrist
"What We Talk About When We Talk About Love,"
    Raymond Carver

Suggestions for what novels to read is a harder assignment. Naturally, it would be splendid if one could read *all* the great books, starting with *Canterbury Tales, Tristam Shandy, Tom Jones, Don Quixote*, all of Shakespeare, *The Red and the Black, Candide*, and so on.

But the ones that I list here are those that I believe will truly help you become a better writer for today's market.

To dig myself further into a hole, I will put asterisks on the books that I think will illustrate what good, clear, vivid, involving, and provocative fiction should be.

And what should be read and reread by you—*immediately*! If you have read them in your youth read them again with a writer's analytical eye. As the late Robertson Davies wrote in *The Enthusiasms of Robertson Davies*:

A truly great book should be read in youth, again in maturity and once more in old age, as a fine building should be seen by morning light, at noon and by moonlight.

I have listed these not chronologically or by their importance, but alphabetically:

The Ambassadors (James)
Anna Karenina (Tolstoy)
Appointment in Samarra (O'Hara)
*The Big Sky (A. B. Guthrie)
Brideshead Revisited (Waugh)
The Brothers Karamazov (Dostoevsky)
The Caine Mutiny (Wouk)
The Call of the Wild (London)
*The Catcher in the Rye (Salinger)
*The Color Purple (Walker)
Crime and Punishment (Dostoevsky)
David Copperfield (Dickens)
*The Day of the Jackal (Forsyth)
Dr. Jekyll and Mr. Hyde (Stevenson)
East of Eden (Steinbeck)
Elmer Gantry (Lewis)
*The End of the Affair (Greene)
The Eustace Diamonds (Trollope)
*Eye of the Needle (Follett)
*A Farewell to Arms (Hemingway)
*The Fifth Business (Davies)
First Love (Turgenev)
Flaubert's Parrot (Julian Barnes)
*For Whom the Bell Tolls (Hemingway)
Frankenstein (Shelley)
*Gone with the Wind (Mitchell)
The Good Earth (Buck)
The Grapes of Wrath (Steinbeck)

The Great Gatsby (Fitzgerald)
A Handful of Dust (Waugh)
 Heart of Darkness (Conrad)
Huckleberry Finn (Twain)
 Ivanhoe (Scott)
 Jane Eyre (C. Brontë)
 Kahawa (Westlake)
 Kim (Kipling)
 Les Miserables (Hugo)
The Moon and Sixpence (Maugham)
 Little Women (Alcott)
Lolita (Nabokov)
 Look Homeward, Angel (Wolfe)
Madame Bovary (Flaubert)
 The Magic Mountain (Mann)
 Main Street (Lewis)
 Miss Lonelyhearts (West)
 Moby-Dick (Melville)
 Native Son (Wright)
 1984 (Orwell)
Of Human Bondage (Maugham)
 The Old Wives' Tale (Bennett)
 A Passage to India (Forster)
 Pride and Prejudice (Austen)
 Rebecca (D. du Maurier)
 The Red Badge of Courage (Crane)
 Return of the Native (Hardy)
 Robinson Crusoe (Defoe)
 Roots (Haley)
 The Scarlet Letter (Hawthorne)
 Shane (Jack Shaeffer)
Shibumi (Trevanian)
 Sons and Lovers (Lawrence)
Stick (Elmore Leonard)
Study in Scarlet (Doyle)

The Sun Also Rises (Hemingway)
Swann's Way (Proust)
Swiss Family Robinson (Wyss)
**Tender Is the Night* (Fitzgerald)
Treasure Island (Stevenson)
The Trick of It (Michael Frayn)
Ulysses (Joyce)
Vanity Fair (Thackeray)
Victory (Conrad)
War and Peace (Tolstoy)
The Way of All Flesh (Butler)
**The Way We Live Now* (Trollope)
What Makes Sammy Run? (Schulberg)
Wuthering Heights (E. Brontë)
**Youngblood Hawke* (Wouk)

Let us end this book with a vibrant thought on the perils and joys of writing by the distinguished novelist Donald Newlove, who came to the Santa Barbara Writers Conference in 1995 and told his audience:

Remember: Writing can get you fed to a lion whose teeth draw your whole face into its foul wet breath and cut your skull with knives. There's no soft way to put this. A black hole swallows you up. Willpower's no help. Getting in print is like beating cancer but losing a lung, staying in print is hopeless. Your best work goes begging. Short stuff has no market. Whatever checks show up—late—you brace at once against the toppling rent and insurance. One by one, your kids in print are pulped, your manuscript trunk feels full of backbreaking author chain, or bodies awaiting Christ, your work's shot down monthly by editors, agents give up on you, and you feed off whatever you write today. *That's* the big loaf that never dies. Today's paragraph comes, a word from the heart of the universe, and shines in the darkness, unquenched.

And you ask for power, wisdom, and love as you make the anvil sing.

INDEX OF AUTHORS
AND TITLES QUOTED

INDEX OF INDIVIDUALS
AND TITLES CITED

ABOUT THE AUTHOR

Artist-author Barnaby Conrad was born in San Francisco, California, in 1922. He studied at the California School of Fine Arts, graduated from Taft Preparatory School in Connecticut, then attended the University of Mexico, where he studied painting and began his career as an amateur bullfighter. After being injured in the bullring he returned to the States, where he continued his studies at Yale, graduating in 1943. He was then named American Vice Consul to Spain, where he served in Seville, Malaga, and Barcelona from 1943 to 1946. While there he performed in many corridas, including one with the great Juan Belmonte. In 1947 he worked as secretary/companion to famed novelist, Sinclair Lewis. In 1949 he studied painting at the Academie Julien in Paris.

Matador, his second novel, was a runaway best-seller and a 1952 Book-of-the-Month Club selection. It remains a classic, having sold some three millions copies, not counting the copies sold in 28 foreign editions. Other books include *Tahiti, La Fiesta Brava, Gates of Fear, The Death of Manolete, San Francisco, Dangerfield, How to Fight a Bull, Famous Last Words, Keepers of the Secret, A Revolting Transaction, Time Is All We have, Hemingway's Spain*, and *The Complete Guide to Writing Fiction*. He has illustrated and done covers for many of these books. His latest work, *Name Dropping*, tells about his San Francisco night spot, El Matador, in the years from 1953 to 1963.

Mr. Conrad is the founder and director of the Santa Barbara Writers Conference, now in its twenty-fourth year.